TEACHER'S GUIDE

W9-ATI-570

Connected Mathematics 2

Thinking With Mathematical Models

Linear and Inverse Variation

Glenda Lappan
James T. Fey
William M. Fitzgerald
Susan N. Friel
Elizabeth Difanis Phillips

Boston, Massachusetts · Glenview, Illinois · Shoreview, Minnesota · Upper Saddle River, New Jersey

Connected Mathematics™ was developed at Michigan State University with financial support from the Michigan State University Office of the Provost, Computing and Technology, and the College of Natural Science.

This material is based upon work supported by the National Science Foundation under Grant No. MDR 9150217 and Grant No. ESI 9986372. Opinions expressed are those of the authors and not necessarily those of the Foundation.

The Michigan State University authors and administration have agreed that all MSU royalties arising from this publication will be devoted to purposes supported by the Department of Mathematics and the MSU Mathematics Enrichment Fund.

13-digit ISBN 978-0-13-366201-6
10-digit ISBN 0-13-366201-2
1 2 3 4 5 6 7 8 9 10 11 10 09 08

Authors of Connected Mathematics

(from left to right) Glenda Lappan, Betty Phillips, Susan Friel, Bill Fitzgerald, Jim Fey

Glenda Lappan is a University Distinguished Professor in the Department of Mathematics at Michigan State University. Her research and development interests are in the connected areas of students' learning of mathematics and mathematics teachers' professional growth and change related to the development and enactment of K–12 curriculum materials.

James T. Fey is a Professor of Curriculum and Instruction and Mathematics at the University of Maryland. His consistent professional interest has been development and research focused on curriculum materials that engage middle and high school students in problem-based collaborative investigations of mathematical ideas and their applications.

William M. Fitzgerald (*Deceased*) was a Professor in the Department of Mathematics at Michigan State University. His early research was on the use of concrete materials in supporting student learning and led to the development of teaching materials for laboratory environments. Later he helped develop a teaching model to support student experimentation with mathematics.

Susan N. Friel is a Professor of Mathematics Education in the School of Education at the University of North Carolina at Chapel Hill. Her research interests focus on statistics education for middle-grade students and, more broadly, on teachers' professional development and growth in teaching mathematics K–8.

Elizabeth Difanis Phillips is a Senior Academic Specialist in the Mathematics Department of Michigan State University. She is interested in teaching and learning mathematics for both teachers and students. These interests have led to curriculum and professional development projects at the middle school and high school levels, as well as projects related to the teaching and learning of algebra across the grades.

CMP2 Development Staff

Teacher Collaborator in Residence
Yvonne Grant
Michigan State University

Production and Field Site Manager
Lisa Keller
Michigan State University

Administrative Assistant
Judith Martus Miller
Michigan State University

Technical and Editorial Support
Brin Keller, Peter Lappan, Jim Laser, Michael Masterson, Stacey Miceli

Assessment Team
June Bailey and **Debra Sobko** (Apollo Middle School, Rochester, New York), **George Bright** (University of North Carolina, Greensboro), **Gwen Ranzau Campbell** (Sunrise Park Middle School, White Bear Lake, Minnesota), **Holly DeRosia, Kathy Dole,** and **Teri Keusch** (Portland Middle School, Portland, Michigan), **Mary Beth Schmitt** (Traverse City East Junior High School, Traverse City, Michigan), **Genni Steele** (Central Middle School, White Bear Lake, Minnesota), **Jacqueline Stewart** (Okemos, Michigan), **Elizabeth Tye** (Magnolia Junior High School, Magnolia, Arkansas)

Development Assistants
At Lansing Community College *Undergraduate Assistant:* **James Brinegar**

At Michigan State University *Graduate Assistants:* **Dawn Berk, Emily Bouck, Bulent Buyukbozkirli, Kuo-Liang Chang, Christopher Danielson, Srinivasa Dharmavaram, Deb Johanning, Wesley Kretzschmar, Kelly Rivette, Sarah Sword, Tat Ming Sze, Marie Turini, Jeffrey Wanko;** *Undergraduate Assistants:* **Daniel Briggs, Jeffrey Chapin, Jade Corsé, Elisha Hardy, Alisha Harold, Elizabeth Keusch, Julia Letoutchaia, Karen Loeffler, Brian Oliver, Carl Oliver, Evonne Pedawi, Lauren Rebrovich**

At the University of Maryland *Graduate Assistants:* **Kim Harris Bethea, Kara Karch**

At the University of North Carolina (Chapel Hill) *Graduate Assistants:* **Mark Ellis, Trista Stearns;** *Undergraduate Assistant:* **Daniel Smith**

Advisory Board for CMP2

Thomas Banchoff
Professor of Mathematics
Brown University
Providence, Rhode Island

Anne Bartel
Mathematics Coordinator
Minneapolis Public Schools
Minneapolis, Minnesota

Hyman Bass
Professor of Mathematics
University of Michigan
Ann Arbor, Michigan

Joan Ferrini-Mundy
Associate Dean of the College of
Natural Science; Professor
Michigan State University
East Lansing, Michigan

James Hiebert
Professor
University of Delaware
Newark, Delaware

Susan Hudson Hull
Charles A. Dana Center
University of Texas
Austin, Texas

Michele Luke
Mathematics Curriculum
Coordinator
West Junior High
Minnetonka, Minnesota

Kay McClain
Assistant Professor of
Mathematics Education
Vanderbilt University
Nashville, Tennessee

Edward Silver
Professor; Chair of Educational
Studies
University of Michigan
Ann Arbor, Michigan

Judith Sowder
Professor Emerita
San Diego State University
San Diego, California

Lisa Usher
Mathematics Resource Teacher
California Academy of
Mathematics and Science
San Pedro, California

Field Test Sites for CMP2

During the development of the revised edition of *Connected Mathematics* (CMP2), more than 100 classroom teachers have field-tested materials at 49 school sites in 12 states and the District of Columbia. This classroom testing occurred over three academic years (2001 through 2004), allowing careful study of the effectiveness of each of the 24 units that comprise the program. A special thanks to the students and teachers at these pilot schools.

Arkansas
Magnolia Public Schools
Kittena Bell*, Judith Trowell*; *Central Elementary School:* Maxine Broom, Betty Eddy, Tiffany Fallin, Bonnie Flurry, Carolyn Monk, Elizabeth Tye; *Magnolia Junior High School:* Monique Bryan, Ginger Cook, David Graham, Shelby Lamkin

Colorado
Boulder Public Schools
Nevin Platt Middle School: Judith Koenig

St. Vrain Valley School District, Longmont
Westview Middle School: Colleen Beyer, Kitty Canupp, Ellie Decker*, Peggy McCarthy, Tanya deNobrega, Cindy Payne, Ericka Pilon, Andrew Roberts

District of Columbia
Capitol Hill Day School: Ann Lawrence

Georgia
University of Georgia, Athens
Brad Findell

Madison Public Schools
Morgan County Middle School: Renee Burgdorf, Lynn Harris, Nancy Kurtz, Carolyn Stewart

Maine
Falmouth Public Schools
Falmouth Middle School: Donna Erikson, Joyce Hebert, Paula Hodgkins, Rick Hogan, David Legere, Cynthia Martin, Barbara Stiles, Shawn Towle*

Michigan
Portland Public Schools
Portland Middle School: Mark Braun, Holly DeRosia, Kathy Dole*, Angie Foote, Teri Keusch, Tammi Wardwell

Traverse City Area Public Schools
Bertha Vos Elementary: Kristin Sak; *Central Grade School:* Michelle Clark; Jody Meyers; *Eastern Elementary:* Karrie Tufts; *Interlochen Elementary:* Mary McGee-Cullen; *Long Lake Elementary:* Julie Faulkner*, Charlie Maxbauer, Katherine Sleder; *Norris Elementary:* Hope Slanaker; *Oak Park Elementary:* Jessica Steed; *Traverse Heights Elementary:* Jennifer Wolfert; *Westwoods Elementary:* Nancy Conn; *Old Mission Peninsula School:* Deb Larimer; *Traverse City East Junior High:* Ivanka Berkshire, Ruthanne Kladder, Jan Palkowski, Jane Peterson, Mary Beth Schmitt; *Traverse City West Junior High:* Dan Fouch*, Ray Fouch

Sturgis Public Schools
Sturgis Middle School: Ellen Eisele

Minnesota
Burnsville School District 191
Hidden Valley Elementary: Stephanie Cin, Jane McDevitt

Hopkins School District 270
Alice Smith Elementary: Sandra Cowing, Kathleen Gustafson, Martha Mason, Scott Stillman; *Eisenhower Elementary:* Chad Bellig, Patrick Berger, Nancy Glades, Kye Johnson, Shane Wasserman, Victoria Wilson; *Gatewood Elementary:* Sarah Ham, Julie Kloos, Janine Pung, Larry Wade; *Glen Lake Elementary:* Jacqueline Cramer, Kathy Hering, Cecelia Morris, Robb Trenda; *Katherine Curren Elementary:* Diane Bancroft, Sue DeWit, John Wilson; *L. H. Tanglen Elementary:* Kevin Athmann, Lisa Becker, Mary LaBelle, Kathy Rezac, Roberta Severson; *Meadowbrook Elementary:* Jan Gauger, Hildy Shank, Jessica Zimmerman; *North Junior High:* Laurel Hahn, Kristin Lee, Jodi Markuson, Bruce Mestemacher, Laurel Miller, Bonnie Rinker, Jeannine Salzer, Sarah Shafer, Cam Stottler; *West Junior High:* Alicia Beebe, Kristie Earl, Nobu Fujii, Pam Georgetti, Susan Gilbert, Regina Nelson Johnson, Debra Lindstrom, Michele Luke*, Jon Sorensen

Minneapolis School District 1
Ann Sullivan K–8 School: Bronwyn Collins; Anne Bartel* (Curriculum and Instruction Office)

Wayzata School District 284
Central Middle School: Sarajane Myers, Dan Nielsen, Tanya Ravnholdt

White Bear Lake School District 624
Central Middle School: Amy Jorgenson, Michelle Reich, Brenda Sammon

New York
New York City Public Schools
IS 89: Yelena Aynbinder, Chi-Man Ng, Nina Rapaport, Joel Spengler, Phyllis Tam*, Brent Wyso; *Wagner Middle School:* Jason Appel, Intissar Fernandez, Yee Gee Get, Richard Goldstein, Irving Marcus, Sue Norton, Bernadita Owens, Jennifer Rehn*, Kevin Yuhas

---

* indicates a Field Test Site Coordinator

Ohio

Talawanda School District, Oxford
Talawanda Middle School: Teresa Abrams, Larry Brock, Heather Brosey, Julie Churchman, Monna Even, Karen Fitch, Bob George, Amanda Klee, Pat Meade, Sandy Montgomery, Barbara Sherman, Lauren Steidl

Miami University
Jeffrey Wanko*

Springfield Public Schools
Rockway School: Jim Mamer

Pennsylvania

Pittsburgh Public Schools
Kenneth Labuskes, Marianne O'Connor, Mary Lynn Raith*; *Arthur J. Rooney Middle School:* David Hairston, Stamatina Mousetis, Alfredo Zangaro; *Frick International Studies Academy:* Suzanne Berry, Janet Falkowski, Constance Finseth, Romika Hodge, Frank Machi; *Reizenstein Middle School:* Jeff Baldwin, James Brautigam, Lorena Burnett, Glen Cobbett, Michael Jordan, Margaret Lazur, Tamar McPherson, Melissa Munnell, Holly Neely, Ingrid Reed, Dennis Reft

Texas

Austin Independent School District
Bedichek Middle School: Lisa Brown, Jennifer Glasscock, Vicki Massey

El Paso Independent School District
Cordova Middle School: Armando Aguirre, Anneliesa Durkes, Sylvia Guzman, Pat Holguin*, William Holguin, Nancy Nava, Laura Orozco, Michelle Peña, Roberta Rosen, Patsy Smith, Jeremy Wolf

Plano Independent School District
Patt Henry, James Wohlgehagen*; *Frankford Middle School:* Mandy Baker, Cheryl Butsch, Amy Dudley, Betsy Eshelman, Janet Greene, Cort Haynes, Kathy Letchworth, Kay Marshall, Kelly McCants, Amy Reck, Judy Scott, Syndy Snyder, Lisa Wang; *Wilson Middle School:* Darcie Bane, Amanda Bedenko, Whitney Evans, Tonelli Hatley, Sarah (Becky) Higgs, Kelly Johnston, Rebecca McElligott, Kay Neuse, Cheri Slocum, Kelli Straight

Washington

Evergreen School District
Shahala Middle School: Nicole Abrahamsen, Terry Coon*, Carey Doyle, Sheryl Drechsler, George Gemma, Gina Helland, Amy Hilario, Darla Lidyard, Sean McCarthy, Tilly Meyer, Willow Nuewelt, Todd Parsons, Brian Pederson, Stan Posey, Shawn Scott, Craig Sjoberg, Lynette Sundstrom, Charles Switzer, Luke Youngblood

Wisconsin

Beaver Dam Unified School District
Beaver Dam Middle School: Jim Braemer, Jeanne Frick, Jessica Greatens, Barbara Link, Dennis McCormick, Karen Michels, Nancy Nichols*, Nancy Palm, Shelly Stelsel, Susan Wiggins

---

* indicates a Field Test Site Coordinator

Reviews of CMP to Guide Development of CMP2

Before writing for CMP2 began or field tests were conducted, the first edition of *Connected Mathematics* was submitted to the mathematics faculties of school districts from many parts of the country and to 80 individual reviewers for extensive comments.

School District Survey Reviews of CMP

Arizona
Madison School District #38 (Phoenix)

Arkansas
Cabot School District, Little Rock School District, Magnolia School District

California
Los Angeles Unified School District

Colorado
St. Vrain Valley School District (Longmont)

Florida
Leon County Schools (Tallahassee)

Illinois
School District #21 (Wheeling)

Indiana
Joseph L. Block Junior High (East Chicago)

Kentucky
Fayette County Public Schools (Lexington)

Maine
Selection of Schools

Massachusetts
Selection of Schools

Michigan
Sparta Area Schools

Minnesota
Hopkins School District

Texas
Austin Independent School District, The El Paso Collaborative for Academic Excellence, Plano Independent School District

Wisconsin
Platteville Middle School

Individual Reviewers of CMP

Arkansas
Deborah Cramer; Robby Frizzell *(Taylor)*; Lowell Lynde *(University of Arkansas, Monticello)*; Leigh Manzer *(Norfork)*; Lynne Roberts *(Emerson High School, Emerson)*; Tony Timms *(Cabot Public Schools)*; Judith Trowell *(Arkansas Department of Higher Education)*

California
José Alcantar *(Gilroy)*; Eugenie Belcher *(Gilroy)*; Marian Pasternack *(Lowman M. S. T. Center, North Hollywood)*; Susana Pezoa *(San Jose)*; Todd Rabusin *(Hollister)*; Margaret Siegfried *(Ocala Middle School, San Jose)*; Polly Underwood *(Ocala Middle School, San Jose)*

Colorado
Janeane Golliher *(St. Vrain Valley School District, Longmont)*; Judith Koenig *(Nevin Platt Middle School, Boulder)*

Florida
Paige Loggins *(Swift Creek Middle School, Tallahassee)*

Illinois
Jan Robinson *(School District #21, Wheeling)*

Indiana
Frances Jackson *(Joseph L. Block Junior High, East Chicago)*

Kentucky
Natalee Feese *(Fayette County Public Schools, Lexington)*

Maine
Betsy Berry *(Maine Math & Science Alliance, Augusta)*

Maryland
Joseph Gagnon *(University of Maryland, College Park)*; Paula Maccini *(University of Maryland, College Park)*

Massachusetts
George Cobb *(Mt. Holyoke College, South Hadley)*; Cliff Kanold *(University of Massachusetts, Amherst)*

Michigan
Mary Bouck *(Farwell Area Schools)*; Carol Dorer *(Slauson Middle School, Ann Arbor)*; Carrie Heaney *(Forsythe Middle School, Ann Arbor)*; Ellen Hopkins *(Clague Middle School, Ann Arbor)*; Teri Keusch *(Portland Middle School, Portland)*; Valerie Mills *(Oakland Schools, Waterford)*; Mary Beth Schmitt *(Traverse City East Junior High, Traverse City)*; Jack Smith *(Michigan State University, East Lansing)*; Rebecca Spencer *(Sparta Middle School, Sparta)*; Ann Marie Nicoll Turner *(Tappan Middle School, Ann Arbor)*; Scott Turner *(Scarlett Middle School, Ann Arbor)*

Minnesota
Margarita Alvarez *(Olson Middle School, Minneapolis)*; Jane Amundson *(Nicollet Junior High, Burnsville)*; Anne Bartel *(Minneapolis Public Schools)*; Gwen Ranzau Campbell *(Sunrise Park Middle School, White Bear Lake)*; Stephanie Cin *(Hidden Valley Elementary, Burnsville)*; Joan Garfield *(University of Minnesota, Minneapolis)*; Gretchen Hall *(Richfield Middle School, Richfield)*; Jennifer Larson *(Olson Middle School, Minneapolis)*; Michele Luke *(West Junior High, Minnetonka)*; Jeni Meyer *(Richfield Junior High, Richfield)*; Judy Pfingsten *(Inver Grove Heights Middle School, Inver Grove Heights)*; Sarah Shafer *(North Junior High, Minnetonka)*; Genni Steele *(Central Middle School, White Bear Lake)*; Victoria Wilson *(Eisenhower Elementary, Hopkins)*; Paul Zorn *(St. Olaf College, Northfield)*

New York
Debra Altenau-Bartolino *(Greenwich Village Middle School, New York)*; Doug Clements *(University of Buffalo)*; Francis Curcio *(New York University, New York)*; Christine Dorosh *(Clinton School for Writers, Brooklyn)*; Jennifer Rehn *(East Side Middle School, New York)*; Phyllis Tam *(IS 89 Lab School, New York)*; Marie Turini *(Louis Armstrong Middle School, New York)*; Lucy West *(Community School District 2, New York)*; Monica Witt *(Simon Baruch Intermediate School 104, New York)*

Pennsylvania
Robert Aglietti *(Pittsburgh)*; Sharon Mihalich *(Freeport)*; Jennifer Plumb *(South Hills Middle School, Pittsburgh)*; Mary Lynn Raith *(Pittsburgh Public Schools)*

Texas
Michelle Bittick *(Austin Independent School District)*; Margaret Cregg *(Plano Independent School District)*; Sheila Cunningham *(Klein Independent School District)*; Judy Hill *(Austin Independent School District)*; Patricia Holguin *(El Paso Independent School District)*; Bonnie McNemar *(Arlington)*; Kay Neuse *(Plano Independent School District)*; Joyce Polanco *(Austin Independent School District)*; Marge Ramirez *(University of Texas at El Paso)*; Pat Rossman *(Baker Campus, Austin)*; Cindy Schimek *(Houston)*; Cynthia Schneider *(Charles A. Dana Center, University of Texas at Austin)*; Uri Treisman *(Charles A. Dana Center, University of Texas at Austin)*; Jacqueline Weilmuenster *(Grapevine-Colleyville Independent School District)*; LuAnn Weynand *(San Antonio)*; Carmen Whitman *(Austin Independent School District)*; James Wohlgehagen *(Plano Independent School District)*

Washington
Ramesh Gangolli *(University of Washington, Seattle)*

Wisconsin
Susan Lamon *(Marquette University, Hales Corner)*; Steve Reinhart *(retired, Chippewa Falls Middle School, Eau Claire)*

Thinking With Mathematical Models
Linear and Inverse Variation

> The Student Edition pages for the Unit Opener follow page 14.

Thinking With Mathematical Models
Linear and Inverse Variation

Goals of the Unit

- Recognize linear and nonlinear patterns from verbal descriptions, tables, and graphs and describe those patterns using words and equations

- Write equations to express linear patterns appearing in tables, graphs, and verbal contexts

- Write a linear equation when given specific information, such as two points or a point and the slope

- Approximate linear data patterns with graph and equation models

- Solve linear equations

- Develop an informal understanding of inequalities

- Write equations describing inverse variation

- Use linear and inverse variation equations to solve problems and to make predictions and decisions

Developing Students' Mathematical Habits

The overall goal of *Connected Mathematics* is to help students develop sound mathematical habits. Through their work in this and other algebra units, students learn important questions to ask themselves about any situation that can be represented and modeled mathematically, such as:

- *What are the key variables in this situation?*

- *What is the pattern relating the variables?*

- *What kind of equation will express the relationship?*

- *How can I use the equation to answer questions about the relationship?*

Overview

Functions and the equations that represent them are invaluable tools for quantitative reasoning throughout the physical, biological, social, and management sciences. Development of student understanding of, and skill with, functions and algebraic equations began with *Variables and Patterns* and *Moving Straight Ahead* in grade 7. This first grade 8 unit reviews linear functions and equations and introduces concepts associated with nonlinear functions—in particular, inverse functions—that will be addressed in subsequent algebra units.

In applying algebra to problem-solving tasks, a critical step is representing relationships in symbolic form so that the tools of algebra can be applied effectively. In some situations, the stated problem conditions can be used to write algebraic equations for functions directly and precisely. In other cases, relationships between key variables are only suggested by data patterns. Such relationships can be approximated by mathematical functions, but cannot be precisely described by them. When algebraic equations are used to represent patterns in data from experiments or surveys, the resulting functions are called *mathematical models* of the underlying relationships. The models can be used to make calculations and to estimate answers to questions about the relationships. One of the central goals of *Thinking With Mathematical Models* is to develop student understanding of, and skill with, elementary aspects of the modeling process.

Two of the simplest and most common types of relationships are *direct variation* and *inverse variation*. Simple direct variation models are those that can be expressed with equations in the form $y = kx$. CMP students are familiar with direct variation (although not by name) as a special case of linear relationships. Specifically, direct variations are linear relationships with y-intercepts of 0. Inverse variation models are those that can be expressed with equations in the form $y = \frac{k}{x}$. This unit introduces inverse variation and helps students develop facility in working with this type of relationship in several common contexts.

Summary of Investigations

Investigation 1

Exploring Data Patterns

The central objectives of this investigation are to refresh student understanding of linear relationships and to contrast linear and nonlinear patterns.

Although students work with inverse and quadratic relationships in this investigation, they are not expected to name these specific types of relationships or to represent them symbolically. Students are formally introduced to inverse relationships in Investigation 3 of this unit and to quadratic relationships in the *Frogs, Fleas, and Painted Cubes* unit.

Investigation 2

Linear Models and Equations

This investigation introduces the idea of using a mathematical model to approximate patterns in data. Students review methods of writing linear equations to match given information and methods for solving linear equations. They also use informal methods to solve inequalities.

Investigation 3

Inverse Variation

The overall goal of Investigation 3 is to acquaint students with inverse variation, one of the fundamental nonlinear patterns of variation. Students should become comfortable with interpreting numeric and graphic patterns associated with inverse variations and representing such relationships with symbolic equations.

Mathematics Background

There are three central mathematical ideas developed in this unit: linear functions, equations, and inequalities; inverse variation; and mathematical modeling.

Linear Functions, Equations, and Inequalities

In the grade 7 unit *Moving Straight Ahead*, students learned to recognize, represent symbolically, and analyze relationships in which a dependent variable changes at a constant rate relative to an independent variable. They learned the connections between the rate of change of y, the equation $y = mx + b$, and the slope of the graph. In particular, they learned that m, the coefficient of x in the equation, indicates the constant ratio:

$$\frac{\text{change in } y}{\text{change in } x}$$

which is the slope of the graph of the equation $y = mx + b$.

The constant term b in $y = mx + b$ indicates the y-intercept of the graph. In other words, the graph crosses the y-axis at the point $(0, b)$.

Many questions about linear functions can be answered by solving equations of the form $c = mx + b$ for x (c is a constant). In *Moving Straight Ahead*, students learned to approximate solutions to such equations by using tables and graphs of (x, y) values. They also learned to find exact solutions by undoing the operations to get $x = (c - b) \div m$ and by using the properties of equality (for example, adding the same quantity to both sides of an equation maintains the equality).

Another way to solve $c = mx + b$ for x is to look at the associated fact families. The concept of fact families highlights the inverse relationship between addition and subtraction and between multiplication and division. Students can interpret subtraction problems as missing addend problems and division problems as missing factor problems. Fact families with whole-number operations are introduced in grade 6, and students revisit them in the grade 7 unit *Accentuate the Negative*. The associated addition and subtraction fact family for $c = mx + b$ is $c = mx + b$, $c - b = mx$, and $c - mx = b$. To solve $c = mx + b$ for x, use the equivalent equation $c - b = mx$. Then look at the associated multiplication/division fact family for this equation. We see that $c - b = mx$ is the same as $(c - b) \div m = x$. So $x = (c - b) \div m$.

Although these basic understandings and skills were addressed in *Moving Straight Ahead*, they need to be revisited and practiced to deepen student understanding. The problems in Investigation 2 of *Thinking With Mathematical Models* are designed to promote this sort of review and extension.

Few real problems that involve linear relationships actually call for the kind of precise answers that occur as solutions to equations. Often, problems call for solutions of inequalities of the form $c \leq mx + b$ or $c \geq mx + b$. Such inequalities have infinitely many solutions The algebraic, numeric, and graphic strategies that lead to solutions of linear inequalities are related to those for equations. However, there are some key differences. For example, you can multiply or divide both sides of an equation by a negative number without changing the solution. However, when you multiply or divide both sides of an inequality by a negative number, the direction of the inequality is reversed. Consider the inequality $5 < 12$. If you multiply both sides by -1, you must reverse the inequality to get $-5 > -12$.

The treatment of inequalities in this unit is informal. We do not introduce algebraic techniques for solving linear inequalities. That topic is addressed in the upcoming unit *The Shapes of Algebra*. Rather, the problems help invite students to become sensitive to the implications of phrases such as "at least" and "at most," to begin using inequality notation to express problem conditions, and to scan tables and graphs to find solutions for inequalities. For instance, the following table and graph suggest that $1.5x + 1 < 7$ for $x < 4$.

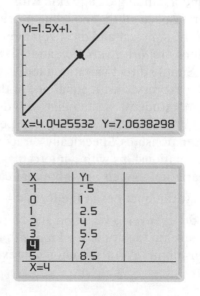

Inverse Variation

The terms *direct variation* and *inverse variation* are used throughout quantitative work in almost every facet of the physical, biological, social, and management sciences. Physicists summarize profound principles with phrases such as, "gravitational attraction of two bodies is directly proportional to the product of their masses and inversely proportional to the square of the distance between their centers of mass."

In everyday language, the phrase "y varies directly with x" means "as x increases, y increases," and "y varies inversely with x" means "as x increases, y decreases." However, the technical meanings of direct variation and inverse variation are more specific than this.

The phrase "y varies directly with x, or is directly proportional to x," means that there is some fixed number k such that $y = kx$. The equation $y = kx$ implies that the ratio $\frac{y}{x}$ is equal to a constant value, k. (This is why the word "proportional" is used in the preceding alternative statement of direct variation.) As long as this proportionality constant k is positive, the pattern of "as x increases, y increases" holds. But there is a particular way that y increases. Specifically, when x increases n times, so does y. So, for example, when x is doubled, y doubles, and when x is tripled, y triples. Note that this is not true for linear relationships of the form $y = kx + b$ for which $b \neq 0$.

An inverse variation is not simply a relationship in which y decreases as x increases. For example, the graphs below show that for both $y = 10 - x$ and $y = \frac{10}{x}$, y decreases as x increases. However, only $y = \frac{10}{x}$ is an inverse variation.

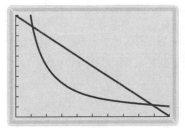

For $y = 10 - x$, y decreases at a constant rate as increasing x-values are subtracted by 10. For $y = \frac{10}{x}$, y decreases at a decreasing rate as 10 is divided by increasing x-values.

For inverse variation, there is a constant k such that $y = \frac{k}{x}$. The inverse variation equation can also be written in the form $xy = k$, which emphasizes that the product of the two variables is constant. In an inverse variation, multiplying x by n multiplies y by $\frac{1}{n}$. So, for example, doubling x halves y, and tripling x multiplies y by $\frac{1}{3}$.

Investigation 3 uses several familiar contexts to develop the concept of inverse variation, building on students' experiences with formulas such as $A = \ell w$ and $d = rt$. The formula $A = \ell w$, for the area of a rectangle, was first explored in the grade 6 unit *Covering and Surrounding*. However, this time, rather than finding the area of a rectangle with a given length and width, as they did in grade 6, students look for combinations of length and width values that give a fixed area. This leads to the formula $\ell = \frac{A}{w}$, which can be used to efficiently calculate such pairs. The formula $d = rt$ relates distance, rate, and time. In earlier units, students calculated the distance traveled for a given rate and time. In this unit, they find combinations of rate and time values that give a fixed distance. This leads to inverse variation equations of the form $r = \frac{d}{t}$ and $t = \frac{d}{r}$, where d is a constant.

Mathematical Modeling

The third key idea of this unit is the notion that the precisely defined objects and operations of mathematics can be used to approximate real-life data patterns that are not as well behaved. In the same sense that a doll or a toy car are models of humans or full-size automobiles, a mathematical function can sometimes be used to model a real-life relationship between variables. For example, the equation $d = 50t$ might make good predictions for the distance traveled as a function of elapsed time. However, this formula will probably not give exact distance values for most specific times, because it is very unlikely that a constant speed can be maintained throughout the trip.

It is important to realize that models are meant to approximate data and may be useful for only a certain range of values. For example, in one ACE exercise, students model the relationship between the age and weight of a Chihuahua based on data for the first few months of a Chihuahua's life. They find that their model is useful for only a limited range of ages because, after a certain age, dogs stop growing.

Using mathematical modeling to solve quantitative problems involves at least five basic steps:

1. Identify the key variables involved in the problem situation.

2. Collect data that indicate the nature of the relationship between those variables.

3. Find an algebraic equation that approximates, or models, the relationship.

4. Use the model to write and solve equations or to make calculations that provide information about values between or beyond the data values.

5. Interpret the results of the mathematical calculations in the context of the original problem.

Effective use of mathematical modeling in solving real problems requires awareness of the overall modeling process and a repertoire of mathematical concepts and skills for model building and analysis. This unit is only a modest introduction to these ideas. It lays a foundation for a more sophisticated and thorough development of modeling strategies in high school and college mathematics and science courses.

Finding a good model for data requires finding a function type with a graph that matches the pattern in a plot of available data. In this unit, students meet only situations in which linear or inverse variation models are particularly appropriate. For the linear examples, students "eyeball" a good fitting line and then use what they know about finding equations for lines to get the function rule. Students do *not* find the "line of best fit" for the data. Finding the line of best fit requires using regression to find the line that *best* matches the data. For the inverse variation examples, we suggest only that students experiment with data plots and test function rules to establish reasonable proportionality constants. Using the plotting and function-graphing capabilities of a graphing calculator makes successive approximation an effective modeling technique. For an introduction to this method, using a TI-83 Plus calculator, see the Technology section on page 10.

Big Idea	Prior Work	Future Work
Recognizing linear and nonlinear patterns in tables and graphs and describing those patterns using words and equations	*Variables and Patterns; Moving Straight Ahead; Comparing and Scaling*	*Growing, Growing, Growing; Frogs, Fleas, and Painted Cubes; Say it With Symbols*
Writing equations to express patterns appearing in tables, graphs, and "stories"	Finding slopes of lines and investigating parallel lines (*Moving Straight Ahead*); formulating, reading, and interpreting symbolic rules (*Moving Straight Ahead; Variables and Patterns*)	*Growing, Growing, Growing; Frogs, Fleas, and Painted Cubes; Say It With Symbols; The Shapes of Algebra*
Solving linear equations	Solving problems in geometric and algebraic contexts (*Shapes and Designs; Covering and Surrounding; Moving Straight Ahead; Variables and Patterns; Comparing and Scaling*)	Solving geometric and algebraic problems (*Frogs, Fleas, and Painted Cubes; Say It With Symbols; Kaleidoscopes, Hubcaps, and Mirrors; The Shapes of Algebra*)
Modeling situations with inequalities	Modeling situations with linear equations (*Moving Straight Ahead; Variables and Patterns; Comparing and Scaling*)	Finding exact solutions of linear inequalities (*The Shapes of Algebra*)
Writing equations to describe inverse variation	Formulating, reading, and interpreting symbolic rules (*Moving Straight Ahead; Variables and Patterns; Comparing and Scaling*)	
Using linear and inverse equations to solve problems and to make predictions		Solving quadratic equations (*Frogs, Fleas, and Painted Cubes; Say It With Symbols*)

Planning for the Unit

Pacing Suggestions and Materials

Investigations and Assessments	Pacing 45–50 min. classes	Materials for Students	Materials for Teachers
1 Exploring Data Patterns	4 days	Colored pens, pencils, or markers; books of the same thickness; a small paper cup; pennies; several $11 \times 4\frac{1}{4}$-inch strips of paper; $4\frac{1}{4}$-inch strips of paper with lengths 4, 6, 8, 9, and 11 inches	Transparencies 1.1 and 1.3; Chart paper and markers (optional)
Mathematical Reflections	$\frac{1}{2}$ day		
Assessment: Check Up 1	$\frac{1}{2}$ day		
2 Linear Models and Equations	5 days	Chart paper and markers (optional); transparent grids and transparency markers (optional); graphing calculators (optional); Labsheet 2ACE Exercise 3	Chart paper and markers (optional); piece of uncooked spaghetti or another thin, straight object; Transparencies 2.1A, 2.1B, 2.2A, 2.2B, and 2.3
Mathematical Reflections	$\frac{1}{2}$ day		
Assessment: Partner Quiz	$\frac{1}{2}$ day		
3 Inverse Variation	5 days	Colored pens, pencils, or markers; chart paper (optional)	Transparencies 3.1A, 3.1B, 3.2A, and 3.2B
Mathematical Reflections	$\frac{1}{2}$ day		
Looking Back and Looking Ahead	$\frac{1}{2}$ day		
Assessment: Self Assessment	Take Home		
Assessment: Unit Test	1 day		

Total Time **18 days**	Materials to Use in All Investigations	
For detailed pacing for Problems within each Investigation, see the Suggested Pacing at the beginning of each Investigation. For pacing with block scheduling, see next page.	Calculators, grid paper, blank transparencies and transparency markers (optional), student notebooks	Blank transparencies and transparency markers (optional)

Pacing for Block Scheduling (90-minute class periods)

Investigation	Suggested Pacing	Investigation	Suggested Pacing	Investigation	Suggested Pacing
Investigation 1	$2\frac{1}{2}$ **days**	**Investigation 2**	**3 days**	**Investigation 3**	$3\frac{1}{2}$ **days**
Problem 1.1	1 day	Problem 2.1	$\frac{1}{2}$ day	Problem 3.1	1 day
Problem 1.2	$\frac{1}{2}$ day	Problem 2.2	1 day	Problem 3.2	1 day
Problem 1.3	$\frac{1}{2}$ day	Problem 2.3	$\frac{1}{2}$ day	Problem 3.3	1 day
Math Reflections	$\frac{1}{2}$ day	Problem 2.4	$\frac{1}{2}$ day	Math Reflections	$\frac{1}{2}$ day
		Math Reflections	$\frac{1}{2}$ day		

Vocabulary

Essential Terms Developed in This Unit	Useful Terms Referenced in This Unit	Terms Developed in Previous Units	
inverse variation	additive inverse	area	profit
linear model	breaking weight	average speed	proportion
mathematical model	demand	coefficient	rate
	direct variation	constant term	rate of change
	multiplicative inverse	coordinate graph	ratio
	supply	coordinate pair	rise
		dependent variable	run
		fact families	scale
		independent variable	scatter plot
		inequality	slope
		length	surface area
		linear equation	table
		linear relationship	variable
		patterns of change	width
		point of intersection	*y*-intercept
		prism	

Program Resources

Go Online
PHSchool.com
For: Teacher Resources
Web Code: apk-5500

Components

Use the chart below to quickly see which components are available for each Investigation.

Investigation	Labsheets	Additional Practice	Transparencies		Formal Assessment		Assessment Options	
			Problem	Summary	Check Up	Partner Quiz	Multiple-Choice	Question Bank
1		✔	1.1, 1.3		✔			
2	2ACE Exercise 3	✔	2.1A, 2.1B, 2.2A, 2.2B, 2.3			✔	✔	✔
3		✔	3.1A, 3.1B, 3.2A, 3.2B			✔	✔	✔
For the Unit		*ExamView* CD-ROM, Web site	LBLA		Unit Test, Notebook Check, Self Assessment		Multiple-Choice, Question Bank, *ExamView* CD-ROM	

Also Available for Use With This Unit
- Parent Guide: take-home letter for the unit
- Implementing CMP

- Spanish Assessment Resources
- Additional online and technology resources

Technology

The Use of Calculators

Connected Mathematics was developed with the belief that calculators should be available and that students should learn when their use is appropriate. For this reason, we do not designate specific problems as "calculator problems." A graphing calculator will be useful in solving a number of the problems in *Thinking with Mathematical Models*.

Calculator Tables

The table feature of a graphing calculator is a powerful tool. You may want to consult your calculator's manual to be certain how to use this feature. On the TI-83 Plus, press $\boxed{Y=}$ and enter an equation, and then press $\boxed{2nd}$ $\boxed{GRAPH}$ to display a table of (x, y) values for that equation. The standard table setting shows x-values in increments of 1. To change this setting, press $\boxed{2nd}$ $\boxed{WINDOW}$ to access the TBLSET screen.

Entering and Plotting Data

You might also introduce the STAT LIST and STAT PLOT functions of the calculator. This is especially appropriate in Problem 2.1. Students can enter the x-coordinates of the points in list 1 (L1) and the y-coordinates in list 2 (L2). They can then use STAT PLOT to specify a scatter plot of (L1, L2) values, choose an appropriate graphing window, and plot the points. To test the fit of a graph model, students can enter its equation and graph it in the same window as the data points. By entering several equations, students can compare different models.

Instructions for plotting points on the TI-83 Plus follow. If your students use a different calculator, consult the manual for instructions on these procedures.

Entering Data To enter a list of (x, y) data pairs, press $\boxed{\text{STAT}}$ to see the screen below.

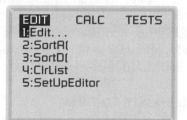

Press $\boxed{\text{ENTER}}$ to select the Edit mode. You will see the screen below. Enter the data pairs into the L1 and L2 columns: Enter the first number and press $\boxed{\text{ENTER}}$; use the arrow keys to change columns; enter the second number, press $\boxed{\text{ENTER}}$; use the arrow keys to return to the L1 column, and so on.

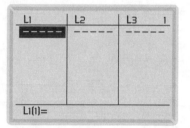

Plotting the Points To plot the data you have entered, press $\boxed{\text{2nd}}$ $\boxed{\text{Y=}}$ to display the STAT PLOTS menu.

Press $\boxed{\text{ENTER}}$ to select Plot1. Use the arrow and $\boxed{\text{ENTER}}$ keys to move around the screen and highlight the elements shown and to specify L1 and L2.

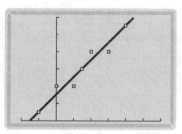

Next, press $\boxed{\text{WINDOW}}$. Adjust the window settings to accommodate the data you have entered.

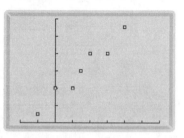

Press $\boxed{\text{GRAPH}}$ to see the plot.

Testing Graph Models

To experiment with equations to find a good model for data set, press $\boxed{\text{Y=}}$ to enter the equation. Then press $\boxed{\text{GRAPH}}$ to display a graph of the equation in the same window as the data points.

Error Messages in Calculator Tables

If the table for an equation is displayed with an x-value for which the equation is undefined, the table will display the word ERROR in the column for the corresponding y-value. You may need to talk with your students about what this means.

Student Interactivity CD-ROM

Includes interactive activities to enhance the learning in the Problems within Investigations.

PHSchool.com

For Students Multiple-choice practice with instant feedback, updated data sources, data sets for Tinkerplots data software.

For Teachers Professional development, curriculum support, downloadable forms, and more.

See also www.math.msu.edu/cmp for more resources for both teachers and students.

ExamView® CD-ROM

Create multiple versions of practice sheets and tests for course objectives and standardized tests. Includes dynamic questions, online testing, student reports, and all test and practice items in Spanish. Also includes all items in the *Assessment Resources* and *Additional Practice*.

Teacher Express™ CD-ROM

Includes a lesson planning tool, the Teacher's Guide pages, and all the teaching resources.

LessonLab Online Courses

LessonLab offers comprehensive, facilitated professional development designed to help teachers implement CMP2 and improve student achievement. To learn more, please visit PHSchool.com/cmp2.

Ongoing Informal Assessment

Embedded in the Student Unit

Problems Use students' work from the Problems to check student understanding.

ACE exercises Use ACE exercises for homework assignments to assess student understanding.

Mathematical Reflections Have students summarize their learning at the end of each Investigation.

Looking Back and Looking Ahead At the end of the unit, use the first two sections to allow students to show what they know about the unit.

Additional Resources

Teacher's Edition Use the Check for Understanding feature of some Summaries and the probing questions that appear in the *Launch*, *Explore*, or *Summarize* sections of all Investigations to check student understanding.

Summary Transparencies Use these transparencies to focus class attention on a summary check for understanding.

Self Assessment

Notebook Check Students use this tool to organize and check their notebooks before giving them to their teacher. Located in *Assessment Resources*.

Self Assessment At the end of the unit, students reflect on and provide examples of what they learned. Located in *Assessment Resources*.

Formal Assessment

Choose the assessment materials that are appropriate for your students.

Assessment	For Use After	Focus	Student Work
Check Up	Invest. 1	Skills	Individual
Partner Quiz	Invest. 2	Rich problems	Pairs
Unit Test	The Unit	Skills, rich problems	Individual

Additional Resources

Multiple-Choice Items Use these items for homework, review, a quiz, or add them to the Unit Test.

Question Bank Choose from these questions for homework, review, or replacements for Quiz, Check Up, or Unit Test questions.

Additional Practice Choose practice exercises for each investigation for homework, review, or formal assessments.

ExamView **CD-ROM** Create practice sheets, review quizzes, and tests with this dynamic software. Give online tests and receive student progress reports. (All test items available in Spanish.)

Spanish Assessment Resources

Includes Partner Quizzes, Check Ups, Unit Test, Multiple-Choice Items, Question Bank, Notebook Check, and Self Assessment. Plus, the *ExamView* CD-ROM has all test items in Spanish.

Correlation to Standardized Tests

Investigation	NAEP	Terra Nova		ITBS	SAT10	Local Test
		CAT6	CTBS			
1 Exploring Data Patterns	D1a, D2e					
2 Linear Models and Equations	A1f, A2a, A2b, A2c, A2d, A4a, A4c, A4d, D1a, D2e					
3 Inverse Variation	A2a, A2b, A3a, D1a, D2e					

NAEP National Assessment of Educational Progress   **CAT6/Terra Nova** California Achievement Test, 6th Ed.   **ITBS** Iowa Test of Basic Skills, Form M
CTBS/Terra Nova Comprehensive Test of Basic Skills   **SAT10** Stanford Achievement Test, 10th Ed.

Using the Unit Opener

Refer students to the three questions posed on the opening page of the student edition. You may want to have a class discussion about these questions, but do not worry about finding the "correct" answer at this time. Each question is posed again in the investigations when the students have learned the mathematical concepts required to answer it. Ask your students to keep these questions in mind as they work through the investigations and to think about how they might use the ideas they are learning to help them determine the answers.

Using the Mathematical Highlights

The Mathematical Highlights page in the student edition provides information to students, parents, and other family members. It gives students a preview of the mathematics and some of the overarching questions that they should ask themselves while studying *Thinking with Mathematical Models*.

As they work through the unit, students can refer back to the Mathematical Highlights page to review what they have learned and to preview what is still to come. This page also tells students' families what mathematical ideas and activities will be covered as the class works through *Thinking with Mathematical Models*.

Connected Mathematics 2

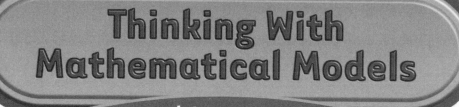

Thinking With Mathematical Models

Linear and Inverse Variation

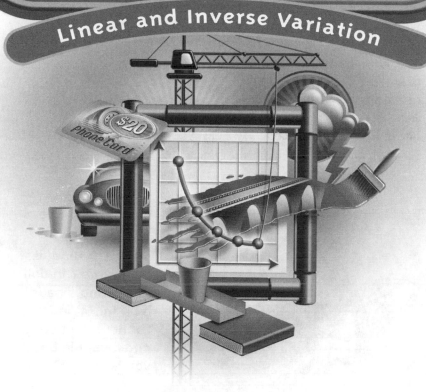

Glenda Lappan

James T. Fey

William M. Fitzgerald

Susan N. Friel

Elizabeth Difanis Phillips

PEARSON

Boston, Massachusetts · Glenview, Illinois · Shoreview, Minnesota · Upper Saddle River, New Jersey

Notes _____

_____

_____

_____

Thinking With Mathematical Models

Linear and Inverse Variation

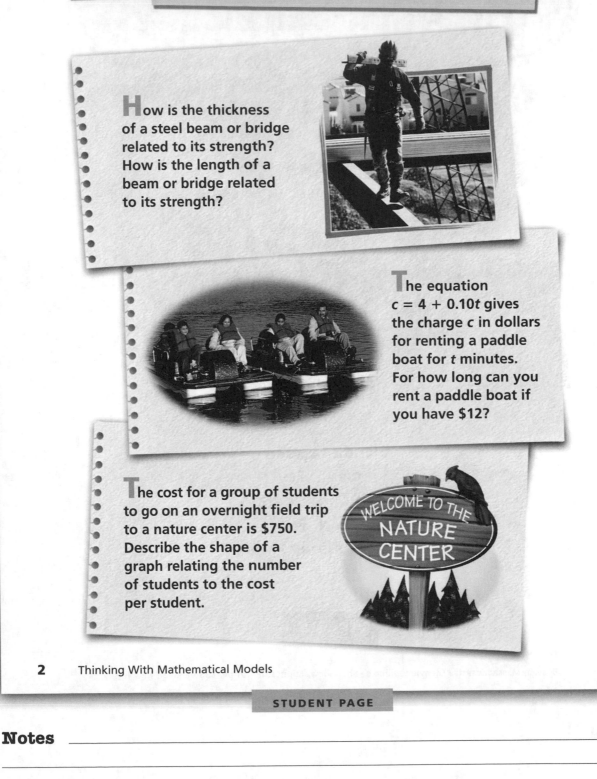

How is the thickness of a steel beam or bridge related to its strength? How is the length of a beam or bridge related to its strength?

The equation $c = 4 + 0.10t$ gives the charge c in dollars for renting a paddle boat for t minutes. For how long can you rent a paddle boat if you have $12?

The cost for a group of students to go on an overnight field trip to a nature center is $750. Describe the shape of a graph relating the number of students to the cost per student.

WELCOME TO THE NATURE CENTER

2 Thinking With Mathematical Models

Notes _____

_____

_____

_____

In earlier *Connected Mathematics* units, you explored relationships between variables. You learned to recognize linear relationships from patterns in tables and graphs and to write equations for such relationships. You then used the equations to help you solve problems. As you work through the investigations in this unit, you will enhance your skill in recognizing and analyzing linear relationships. You will also compare linear patterns with nonlinear patterns, focusing on a special type of nonlinear relationship called an *inverse variation*.

You will conduct experiments, analyze the data, and then write equations that summarize, or model, the data patterns. You will then use your equations to make predictions about values beyond and between the data you collected.

The skills you develop in this unit will help you answer questions like those on the facing page.

Notes _____

_____

_____

_____

Mathematical Highlights

Linear and Inverse Variation

In *Thinking With Mathematical Models,* you will model relationships with graphs and equations, and then use your models to analyze situations and solve problems.

You will learn how to:

- Recognize linear and nonlinear patterns in tables and graphs
- Describe data patterns using words and symbols
- Write equations to express patterns appearing in tables, graphs, and problems
- Solve linear equations
- Model situations with inequalities
- Write equations to describe inverse variations
- Use linear and inverse variation equations to solve problems and to make predictions and decisions

As you work on problems in this unit, ask yourself questions about problem situations that involve related variables.

What are the key variables in this situation?

What is the pattern relating the variables?

What kind of equation will express the relationship?

How can I use the equation to answer questions about the relationship?

Notes _____

_____

_____

_____

Investigation 1 · Exploring Data Patterns

Mathematical and Problem-Solving Goals

- Make tables and graphs to represent data
- Describe relationships between variables
- Use data patterns to make predictions
- Compare and contrast linear and nonlinear relationships

Summary of Problems

Problem 1.1 Testing Bridge Thickness

Students explore a linear relationship as they test how bridge thickness is related to strength. They display their collected data in a table and graph, look for patterns, and use the patterns to make predictions.

Problem 1.2 Testing Bridge Lengths

Students explore a nonlinear relationship as they test how bridge length is related to strength. They look for patterns in their collected data and use the patterns to make predictions.

Problem 1.3 Custom Construction Parts

Students look for differences in the patterns of change for a linear relationship and a nonlinear relationship.

	Suggested Pacing	Materials for Students	Materials for Teachers	ACE Assignments
All	$4\frac{1}{2}$ days	Calculators; colored pens, pencils, or markers; blank transparencies and transparency markers (optional); student notebooks	Blank transparencies and transparency markers (optional)	
1.1	$1\frac{1}{2}$ days	Books of the same thickness; small paper cups; 50 pennies (per group); $11 \times 4\frac{1}{4}$-inch strips of paper; chalk or tape	Transparency 1.1, chart paper; markers (optional)	1, 7–15
1.2	1 day	Books of the same thickness; small paper cups; 50 pennies (per group); $4\frac{1}{4}$-inch strips of paper with lengths 4, 6, 8, 9, and 11 inches; chalk or tape	Chart paper and markers (optional)	2, 16–22
1.3	$1\frac{1}{2}$ days		Transparency 1.3	3–6, 23–34
MR	$\frac{1}{2}$ day			

Testing Bridge Thickness

Goals

- Make tables and graphs to represent data
- Describe relationships between variables
- Use data patterns to make predictions

In their previous work in *Variables and Patterns* and *Moving Straight Ahead*, students explored relationships between variables. They represented relationships in graphs and tables, and used patterns to help them express those relationships as equations. In this problem, students collect data, search for patterns in graphs and tables of the data, and use those patterns to make predictions.

Launch 1.1

For demonstration in the launch, prepare a set of paper strips in advance, folding up the sides as explained in the student edition. Consider whether you want to spend class time having groups fold their own strips or whether you want to prepare the strips for them. The strips need to be folded carefully, which takes time to do well.

Review with students how to decide which variable in a relationship is the *independent variable* and which is the *dependent variable*. Students should ask themselves if the values of one variable depend on the values of the other. In this experiment, the number of pennies a bridge will hold depends on the bridge's thickness. Therefore, the number of pennies, or breaking weight, is the dependent variable. Remind students that the dependent variable is shown on the *y*-axis, and the independent variable is shown on the *x*-axis.

Suggested Questions To introduce the context, have a discussion about the design and strength of bridges.

- *Have you ever walked across a shaky bridge and wondered if it would hold your weight?*

- *Do you get nervous when a car, bus, or train you are in crosses a high bridge?*

- *How do you suppose bridge designers know which materials will give a bridge the strength it needs?*

Discuss the questions in the Getting Ready.

- *How do you think the thickness of a beam is related to its strength?* (Most students will say that thicker beams are stronger.) *Do you think the relationship is linear?* (Answers will vary.)

- *What other variables might affect the strength of a bridge?* (Possible answers: the material the bridge is made of, the length of the bridge)

You may need to review the idea of a *linear relationship*. Ask volunteers to remind the class about the patterns of change in a table and graph of a linear relationship. Discuss the fact that a linear relationship has a constant rate of change. That is, as the values of the independent variable increase by equal amounts, so do the values of the dependent variable. The graph of a linear relationship is a straight line.

Tell students they will conduct an experiment to explore how the strength of a bridge changes as its thickness increases.

With the help of one or two students, demonstrate the experiment, using a single strip of paper.

Suggested Questions Talk with the class about the mechanics of the experiment.

- *Why is it important that the ends of the bridge always overlap the books by 1 inch?* (Because for the comparisons to be meaningful, all of the bridges must be suspended in the same way.)

- *Where should you place the cup?* (in the center of the bridge)

- *How should you add the pennies?* (carefully, using the same technique each time)

- *Should you reuse a paper bridge after it has collapsed?* (No; once a bridge has collapsed, the paper is structurally different from unused paper strips and would give different results.)

Fold a new bridge, but use a sloppy technique. Hold it up for the class to see.

- *Does it matter whether we fold the paper strips the same way every time?* (Yes; to get good results from an experiment, you need to keep everything as consistent as possible.)

- *Would it make a difference if you used a bridge that looked like this? (Yes; it would probably give you data that is very different than if you used a bridge that is folded neatly.)*

- *What might a bridge like this do to your results?* (make your results vary too much)

When the class has an idea of how to conduct the experiment, talk about the data they will collect.

- *We need to agree on a definition before we begin. What does it mean for a bridge to "collapse"?*

For groups to be able to compare their results, students will need to judge the collapse of a bridge in the same way. Many teachers use the point when the bridge touches the table. Some use the point when the bridge first begins to bend. Others have students suspend the bridge high above the table and count the falling of the cup and pennies as the collapse. Also, to compare their results, students should all use books of the same thickness. The experiment works best if the books are at least 1 inch thick. This makes it easier for students to tell when the bridges have collapsed.

Have students conduct the experiment and answer the questions in groups of three or four.

Explore 1.1

Groups may want to assign each student a specific role. For example,

- one student manages the paper

- one student checks that the ends of the bridges overlap each book by 1 inch and that the cup is positioned at the center of the bridge

- one student adds the pennies

- one student records the data

You might suggest that students use chalk or tape to make a mark 1 inch from the end of each book. This will ensure that they set up the bridge the same way every time. They can also mark the center of the top layer of each bridge to help them place the cup.

Ask each student to draw a graph of their group's data. Groups should discuss which variable should be on the horizontal axis and which should be on the vertical axis.

Suggested Questions

- *Which is the independent variable and which is the dependent variable?* (Thickness is the independent variable and should be on the horizontal axis. Breaking weight is the dependent variable and should be on the vertical axis.)

- *What patterns do you see in the data?* (The data appear to be almost linear.)

- *How should your data compare to other groups in the class?* (If they did the experiment in a similar way, then their results should be similar.)

You may want to distribute blank transparencies for some groups to record their findings for sharing during the summary.

Make axes for the graph on a transparency or chart paper and have each group add their data points to create a class scatter plot. (This plot will have several points for each thickness value.)

Summarize 1.1

If some groups put their work on transparencies, ask them to display their results.

Suggested Questions

- *Compare your group's results and predictions with those shown here. What similarities and differences do you see?*

The data will vary slightly from group to group, and groups may have used different methods to make their predictions. Talk about the various methods used.

- *For each layer you added to the bridge, what was the approximate increase in the number of pennies it would hold?*

- *Was the increase in the number of pennies constant? If not, how did you make your predictions for other bridge thicknesses?*

Students will probably have used a formal or informal averaging procedure based on their reasoning that the rate of increase should be constant. If some students used different methods, have them share their ideas. They may offer some interesting rationales.

Discuss the scatter plot of the combined class data. This graph allows students to see the general trend and shows places where the data collected by an individual group is very different than the majority of the data. Discuss why such differences may have occurred. For example, the group may have used a collapsed bridge or may have set up the bridge incorrectly.

Have students save the data they collected and their graphs. In Investigation 2, they will fit a linear model to the data.

1.1 Testing Bridge Thickness

Mathematical Goals

- Make tables and graphs to represent data
- Describe relationships between variables
- Use data patterns to make predictions

Launch

Prepare a set of paper strips as explained in the Student Edition.

Review the concepts of independent and dependent variables.

Have a brief discussion about the design and strength of bridges.

- *Have you ever walked across a shaky bridge and wondered if it would hold your weight?*
- *Do you get nervous when a car, bus, or train you are in crosses a high bridge?*
- *How do you suppose bridge designers know which materials will give a bridge the strength it needs?*

Discuss the Getting Ready questions.

Review the idea of a linear relationship.

Demonstrate the experiment.

- *Why is it important that the ends of the bridge always overlap the books by 1 inch?*
- *Where should you place the cup?*
- *How should you add the pennies?*
- *Should you reuse a paper bridge after it has collapsed?*

Fold a new bridge, but use a sloppy technique and hold it up.

- *Does it matter whether we fold the paper strips the same way every time?*
- *Would it make a difference if you used a bridge that looked like this?*
- *What might a bridge like this do to your results?*

Agree, as a class, on what it means for a paper bridge to collapse.

Have students work in groups of three or four.

Materials

- Transparency 1.1
- Chart paper and markers (optional)

Explore

Suggest that each student play a different role in the bridge experiment.

Ask each student to draw a graph of his or her data.

- *Which is the independent variable and which is the dependent variable?*
- *What patterns do you see in the data?*
- *How should your data compare to other groups in the class?*

Make axes for the graph on a transparency or chart paper and have each group add their data points to create a class scatter plot.

Materials

- Books of the same thickness
- Small paper cups
- Pennies (50 per group)
- 11 × 4¼-inch strips of paper
- Chalk or tape

Ask different groups to display their results.

- *Compare your group's results and predictions with those shown here. What similarities and differences do you see?*

- *For each layer you added to the bridge, what was the approximate increase in the number of pennies it would hold?*

- *Was the increase in the number of pennies constant? If not, how did you make your predictions for other bridge thicknesses?*

Discuss the scatter plot of the combined class data.

Materials
- Student notebooks

ACE Assignment Guide for Problem 1.1

Differentiated Instruction
Solutions for All Learners

Core 1
Other *Connections* 7–15

Adapted For suggestions about adapting Exercise 1 and other ACE exercises, see the *CMP Special Needs Handbook*.
Connecting to Prior Units 7–8: *Comparing and Scaling*; 9: *Covering and Surrounding*; 10: *Covering and Surrounding, Bits and Pieces II, Comparing and Scaling*; 11: *Comparing and Scaling*; 12–15: *Moving Straight Ahead*

Answers to Problem 1.1

A. Answers will vary based on experimental data. Sample:

Bridge-Thickness Experiment

Thickness (layers)	1	2	3	4	5
Breaking Weight (pennies)	9	16	24	34	42

B. Possible graph:

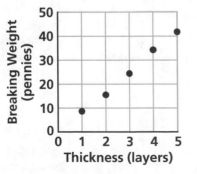

Bridge-Thickness Experiment

C. The relationship is approximately linear. In the table, this is shown by the near-constant differences in breaking weights for consecutive thickness values. In the graph, this is shown by the near straight-line pattern of points. The relationship is also increasing. That is, as the thickness increases, the breaking weight increases.

D. Based on the previous data, one possible prediction is 20 pennies. As thickness increases by 1 layer, the breaking weight increases by about 8 pennies. So as thickness increases by half a layer, breaking weight should increase by about 4 pennies.

E. 1. Based on the data above, one possible prediction is 50 pennies. As thickness increases by 1 layer, the breaking weight increases by about 8 pennies. Therefore, 6 layers would probably have a breaking weight of $42 + 8 = 50$ pennies.

2. Possible answer: The breaking weight is probably not actually a whole number of pennies. Also, the rate of change is not exactly 8 pennies every time, so predictions of the last value of 42 plus 8 might not match the actual breaking weight.

1.2 Testing Bridge Lengths

Goals

- Make tables and graphs to represent data
- Describe relationships between variables
- Use data patterns to make predictions

In this problem, students encounter a nonlinear relationship. They will not be expected to find an equation for the relationship in this experiment.

Launch 1.2

Prepare a set of paper strips in advance. Consider whether you want to spend class time having each group fold their own strips or whether you want to fold the strips for them.

Read with students about the experiment.

Suggested Questions Ask:

- *What do you expect will happen in this experiment?*
- *You are using equipment similar to the equipment you used before. What are the variables this time?* (length and breaking weight)
- *What do you think the data will look like? What shape do you think the graph will have?*

You might have students sketch their predicted graphs, and then share some of these on the board or overhead. Students will probably guess that longer bridges will not support as much weight and that the relationship will be linear. Talk about the reasoning behind their conjectures, but let them discover the actual shape from the experiment.

As in Problem 1.1, establish what it means for a bridge to collapse and discuss ways to minimize variability, such as marking the books to indicate where the strips will be placed, marking the strips to indicate where the cup will be placed, and using a consistent method for adding pennies to the cup. In addition, labeling each strip with its length will help students avoid errors in recording.

Have students work in pairs on the problem, but have each student write up results individually. Be sure that students rest the entire base of the cup on the bridge for accurate results.

Explore 1.2

Have students do the experiment and discuss the questions with their partners, but ask each student to make a table and a graph and to write his or her own answers. You might have pairs put their tables and graphs on large sheets of paper for sharing in the summary.

Have groups record their results in a class scatter plot as they did in Problem 1.1.

Suggested Questions Ask students about their data:

- *Is there a pattern to your data?*
- *Is the pattern similar to the one in the experiment in Problem 1.1?*

Summarize 1.2

If students have put their results on large sheets of paper, ask them to display their work. Have several pairs explain the reasoning behind their work.

Suggested Questions While asking these questions, it may be easier to focus students on the scatter plot of the combined class data.

- *Are there similarities in the results of the different groups? Are there differences? What might have caused those differences?*
- *As bridge length increases, what happens to the number of pennies the bridge can support?* (It decreases.)
- *As bridge length decreases, what happens to the number of pennies the bridge can support?* (It increases.)

Focus the class's attention on this inverse relationship.

- *What shape or pattern do you see in your graph? Are the data linear?* (No; the points form a curve.)
- *How can you tell from your table that the graph will be curved?* (The difference between consecutive breaking weights decreases by less and less as the length increases. The change is not constant.)

Another way to help students see that the data are not linear is to ask about the *x*-intercept.

- *If this were a linear relationship, then the graph would eventually cross the x-axis. What would be the meaning of the point where this happens?* (The bridge of that length would break with no pennies on it.)

You might sketch a linear graph to illustrate this.

- *Does this make sense in this situation?* (no)

Ask students to explain how they determined breaking weights for lengths of 3, 5, 10, and 12 inches. If they are making predictions based on a linear relationship, challenge this idea; the collected data are not linear. It is reasonable, however, to assume that the relationship is linear between each pair of collected data values. For example, if the points for lengths of 4 inches and 6 inches are (4, 42) and (6, 26), then it is reasonable to estimate that the breaking weight for a bridge of length 5 inches is halfway between 26 and 42. It is not reasonable to extrapolate this rate of 8 pennies per inch beyond this interval, however.

Note to the Teacher The data gathered in the bridge-length experiment conform to an inverse relationship. However, because this is experimental data, results will probably vary widely from group to group.

Have students save the data they collected and their graphs. They will examine their data again in Investigation 3, when they are formally introduced to inverse variation.

Mathematical Goals

- Make tables and graphs to represent data
- Describe relationships between variables
- Use data patterns to make predictions

Launch

Prepare a set of paper strips in advance. Read with students about the experiment.

- *What do you expect to happen in this experiment?*
- *You are using equipment similar to the equipment you used before. What are the variables this time?*
- *What do you think the data will look like? What shape do you think the graph will have?*

Talk about the reasoning behind students' conjectures, but let them discover the actual shape from their experimentation.

Remind the class what it means for a bridge to collapse and discuss ways to minimize variability.

Have students work in pairs on the problem, but have each student write up results individually.

Materials
- Books of the same thickness
- Small paper cups
- Pennies (50 per group)
- $4\frac{1}{4}$-inch-wide strips of paper with lengths 4, 6, 8, 9, and 11 inches
- Chalk or tape

Explore

Ask each student to make a table and a graph and to write his or her own answers. Have pairs put their tables and graphs on large sheets of paper for sharing in the summary. Have groups record their results in a class scatter plot as they did in Problem 1.1.

- *Is there a pattern to your data?*
- *Is the pattern similar to the one in the experiment in Problem 1.1?*

Summarize

Display student work. Focus students on the scatter plot of combined class data.

- *Are there similarities in the results of the different groups? Are there differences? What might have caused those differences?*
- *As bridge length increases, what happens to the number of pennies the bridge can support?*
- *As bridge length decreases, what happens to the number of pennies the bridge can support?*

Focus the class's attention on this inverse relationship.

- *What shape or pattern do you see in your graph? Are the data linear?*

Materials
- Student notebooks

continued on next page

Summarize

continued

- *How can you tell from your table that the graph will be curved?*
- *If this were a decreasing linear relationship, then the graph would eventually cross the x-axis. What would be the meaning of the point where this happens? Does this make sense in this situation?*

Ask students how they determined breaking weights for lengths of 3, 5, 10, and 12 inches.

ACE Assignment Guide for Problem 1.2

Differentiated Instruction
Solutions for All Learners

Core 2
Other *Connections* 16–22; unassigned choices from earlier problems

Adapted For suggestions about adapting ACE exercises, see the *CMP Special Needs Handbook*.
Connecting to Prior Units 16–22: *Moving Straight Ahead*

Answers to Problem 1.2

A. Answers will vary. Figure 1 shows the data collected in one class.

B. Graphs will vary. This is the graph of the data in Figure 1.

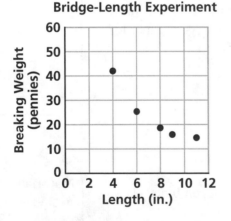

Bridge-Length Experiment

C. Possible answer: As length increases, breaking weight decreases, but the relationship is not linear. In the table, the breaking weights decrease as the lengths increase, but not at a constant rate. In the graph, the pattern of points is a curve that decreases at a slower and slower rate.

D. Predictions and explanations will vary. Students may estimate using the pattern in either the graph or the table. Based on the graph in B, we might predict that the breaking weights are 58, 34, 15, and 13, respectively. The results might not match exactly because the actual breaking weights might not be whole pennies. Whole pennies might be too "coarse" a unit of measure.

E. Possible answer: They are similar in that breaking weight depends on another variable—either bridge thickness or bridge length. However, the nature of the two relationships is very different. As thickness increases, breaking weight increases. As length increases, breaking weight decreases. Furthermore, the relationship between bridge thickness and breaking weight appears to be roughly linear, while the relationship between bridge length and breaking weight does not.

Figure 1   **Bridge-Length Experiment**

Length (in.)	4	6	8	9	11
Breaking Weight (pennies)	42	26	19	16	14

1.3 Custom Construction Parts

Goals

- Make tables and graphs to represent data
- Describe relationships between variables
- Use data patterns to make predictions
- Compare and contrast linear and nonlinear relationships

Launch 1.3

Introduce students to Custom Steel Products (CSP). Explain that the company provides lightweight beams of any size for use as building materials.

Draw 1-foot, 2-foot, and 7-foot beams (as shown below) on the board or overhead, or have students look at the drawings in their books. Help students understand that the length of the base of the beam is considered to be the length of the beam. Also, help them distinguish the beams from the steel rods from which the beams are made.

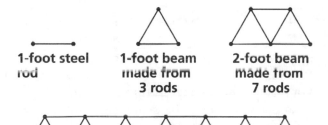

1-foot steel rod   1-foot beam made from 3 rods   2-foot beam made from 7 rods

7-foot beam made from 27 rods

Suggested Questions Ask:

- *What does the 1-foot beam look like?* (an equilateral triangle with 1-foot sides)

- *What does the 2-foot beam look like?* (an isosceles trapezoid in which the longer base is 2 ft long and the shorter base is 1 ft long)

- *What does the 7-foot beam look like?* (an isosceles trapezoid in which the longer base is 7 ft long and the shorter base is 6 ft long)

You might get students started on making the table for Question A. See Transparency 1.3.

- *How many steel rods are in a 1-foot beam?* (3)

- *How many steel rods are in a 2-foot beam?* (7)

If students have trouble seeing the seven rods, point to each rod in the drawing as students count aloud.

- *How many steel rods are in a 7-foot beam?* (27)

- *Do you see any patterns so far?*

Students may begin to make conjectures about how many rods are in a 3-foot beam, and they may correctly guess that this is a linear relationship.

Explain to students that Custom Steel Products also makes staircase frames. Draw 1-step, 2-step, and 3-step frames, as shown below, or have students look at the drawings in their books.

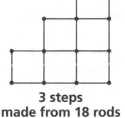

1 step made from 4 rods   2 steps made from 10 rods

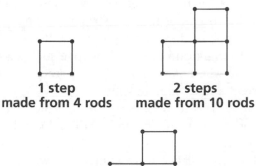

3 steps made from 18 rods

You might help students start the table in Question B.

- *How many rods are in a 1-step frame? (4)*

- *How many rods are in a 2-step frame? (10) How many are in a 3-step frame? (18)*

- *Do you see any patterns in the data?*

Because the relationship between the number of steps and the number of rods is not linear, students may not yet be able to pick out a pattern.

Arrange students in groups of two or three to work on the problem. Make sure each student creates his or her own graphs and tables. Have students prepare a way to share their work with the whole class (such as a transparency or chart paper).

INVESTIGATION 1

Give students time to look for patterns in Question A. There are many ways to count the rods in a beam of a given length. For example,

- A 5-foot beam has 5 rods along the bottom, 4 rods along the top, and 5 pairs of rods joining the top to the bottom. In general, a b-foot beam has b rods along the bottom, $b - 1$ rods along the top, and $2 \times b$ rods joining the top to the bottom.

- A 1-foot beam has 3 rods. To get a 2-foot beam, you add 4 rods; to get a 3-foot beam, you add 4 rods to the 2-foot beam; to get a 4-foot beam, you add 4 rods to the 3-foot beam; and so on. In general, for a b-foot beam, you start with 3 rods and add $4(b - 1)$ rods.

You may want to suggest one of these strategies to groups that are struggling. You might also use one of these strategies to challenge a group to think differently. Challenge such a group to decide whether the strategy is correct or incorrect and to explain why.

Make sure students recognize that the relationship between beam length and number of rods is linear. Ask how they can tell from the table and the graph. Encourage students to write equations for these relationships, and ask how the equations indicate that the relationship is linear.

In Question B, students will probably need to draw more staircases before they see any patterns.

If students are having difficulty seeing patterns, invite them to look at the problem recursively. Use the diagram that follows.

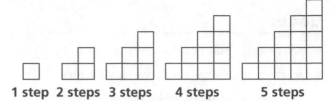

1 step 2 steps 3 steps 4 steps 5 steps

- *How many rods do you need to build 1 step?* (4)

- *How many more rods do you need to build 2 steps?* (6 more, for a total of 10)

- *How many more rods do you need to build 3 steps?* (8 more, for a total of 18)

- *How many more rods do you need to build 4 steps?* (10 more, for a total of 28)

- *Do you see any patterns that can help you?* (You need 4 more rods, then 6 more, then 8 more, then 10 more, and so on. The numbers of rods you add are sequential even numbers.)

Some students may see the pattern as shown in Figure 2.

Or students may see the pattern this way:

1 step:	$4 = 4$
2 steps:	$4 + 6 = 10$
3 steps:	$4 + 6 + 8 = 18$
4 steps:	$4 + 6 + 8 + 10 = 28$
5 steps:	$4 + 6 + 8 + 10 + 12 = 40$

For n steps, the number of rods is the sum of n consecutive even numbers, starting with 4.

There are many, many ways to see patterns in this problem. Make sure students understand that this relationship is not linear. Students do not need to find an equation to represent the relationship.

Figure 2

1 step: 4

2 steps: $4 + (2 \times 3)$

3 steps: $4 + (2 \times 3) + (2 \times 3) + (\mathbf{1} \times 2)$

4 steps: $4 + (2 \times 3) + (2 \times 3) + (1 \times 2) + (2 \times 3) + (\mathbf{2} \times 2)$

5 steps: $4 + (2 \times 3) + (2 \times 3) + (1 \times 2) + (2 \times 3) + (2 \times 2) + (2 \times 3) + (\mathbf{3} \times 2)$

6 steps: $4 + (2 \times 3) + (2 \times 3) + (1 \times 2) + (2 \times 3) + (2 \times 2) + (2 \times 3) + (3 \times 2)$
            $+ (2 \times 3) + (\mathbf{4} \times 2)$

The number of rods for n steps is the number for $n - 1$ steps, plus $(2 \times 3) + [(n - 2) \times 2]$.

Note to the Teacher Note that the number of rods in an n-step frame is $n^2 + 3n$. To understand why, see Figure 3.

Summarize 1.3

Invite students to present their patterns for Question A.

- *Is this relationship linear?* (yes)

- *How do you know by looking at the graph?* (The points fall on a straight line.)

- *How do you know by looking at the table?* (The rate of change is constant; each time the length increases by 1, the number of rods increases by 4.)

- *How is any linear relationship represented in a table?* (As x increases at a constant rate, so does y.) *In a graph?* (by a straight line) *In an equation?* (by the form $y = mx + b$, where b is the y-intercept and m is the rate of change)

Invite students to present their patterns for Question B.

- *Is this relationship linear?* (no)

- *How do you know by looking at the graph?* (The points fall on a curve.)

- *How do you know by looking at the table?* (The rate of change is not constant; as the number of steps increases by 1, the number of rods needed to make the next frame in the pattern increases by a greater and greater amount.)

- *How are these relationships similar to and different from those in the bridge experiments?* (The bridge-thickness relationship is linear, just like the beam relationship. Neither the bridge-length relationship nor the staircase relationship is linear.)

If students are ready to think about equations, discuss strategies for solving linear equations as a review of the grade 7 unit *Moving Straight Ahead.* You might use ACE Exercises 16–18 as part of this discussion.

Figure 3

1 step:	4
2 steps:	4 + (4 + 2)
3 steps:	4 + (4 + 2) + (4 + 2 + 2)
4 steps:	4 + (4 + 2) + (4 + 2 + 2) + (4 + 2 + 2 + 2)
n steps:	4 + (4 + 2) + (4 + 2 + 2) + (4 + 2 + 2 + 2) + ... + (4 + 2 + 2 + ...2)

$$\underbrace{}_{(n - 1)2s}$$

So the number of rods in n steps is:

$$4n + 2 + 2 \times 2 + 3 \times 2 + (n - 1) \times 2 = 4n + 2(n - 1 + n - 2 + n - 3 + ... + 1)$$

We know that $(n - 1) + (n - 2) + (n - 3) + ... + = \dfrac{(n - 1)n}{2}$. (Students will derive this in the unit *Frogs, Fleas, and Painted Cubes.)* Therefore, the number of rods in n steps is:

$$4n + 2 \times \frac{(n - 1)n}{2} = 4n + n^2 - n = n^2 + 3n$$

1.3 Custom Construction Parts

PACING $1\frac{1}{2}$ days

Mathematical Goals

- Make tables and graphs to represent data
- Describe relationships between variables
- Use data patterns to make predictions
- Compare and contrast linear and nonlinear relationships

Launch

Introduce the problem context. Draw 1-foot, 2-foot, and 7-foot beams. Ask students to describe the beams.

Help students start the table for Question A.

- *Do you see any patterns so far?*

Draw the first few staircases. Help students start the Question B table.

- *Do you see any patterns in the data?*

Arrange students in groups of two or three to work on the problem.

Materials
- Transparency 1.3

Explore

Give students a chance to look for patterns in Question A.

In Question B, students will probably need to draw more staircases before they see any patterns. If students are having difficulty seeing a pattern, invite them to look at the problem recursively.

- *How many steel rods do you need to build one step?*
- *How many more rods do you need to build two steps?*
- *How many more do you need to build three steps?*
- *How many more do you need to build four steps?*
- *Do you see any patterns there that can help you?*

There are many, many ways to see patterns in this problem. Make sure students understand that this relationship is not linear.

Summarize

Have students present their patterns for Question A.

- *Is this relationship linear? How can you tell from the graph and table?*

Invite students to present their patterns for Question B.

- *Is this relationship linear?*
- *How do you know by looking at the graph? How do you know by looking at the table?*
- *How are these relationships similar to and different from those in the bridge experiments?*

Materials
- Student notebooks

ACE Assignment Guide for Problem 1.3

Core 3–6
Other *Connections* 23–31; *Extensions* 32–34; unassigned choices from previous problems

Adapted For suggestions about adapting ACE exercises, see the *CMP Special Needs Handbook*.
Connecting to Prior Units 23–26: *Moving Straight Ahead*; 27–29: *Accentuate the Negative*; 30, 31: *Filling and Wrapping*

Answers to Problem 1.3

A. 1. (Figure 4)

2.

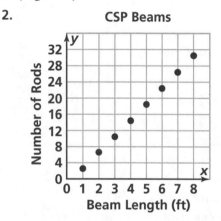

CSP Beams

3. Every time another foot is added to the length, 4 rods are added.

4. In the table, each increase of 1 ft in the beam length yields an increase of 4 in the number of rods. The graph is a straight line. To get from one point to the next, you move over 1 and up 4.

5. 199 rods; explanations will vary.

B. 1. (Figure 5)

2.

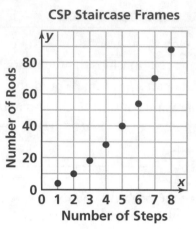

CSP Staircase Frames

3. Possible answer: As you increase the number of steps by 1, the number of rods increases by the next even number.

4. In the table, the number of rods increases by 6, 8, 10, and so on. The graph curves upward at an increasing rate.

5. 180 rods

C. Both patterns are increasing. The beam relationship is linear, so it has a straight-line graph and a table with constant differences. The staircase relationship is nonlinear, so it has a curved graph and a table in which the differences are nonconstant. Both graphs increase from left to right.

D. The beam and bridge-thickness relationships are both increasing and linear. The bridge-length and staircase relationships are both nonlinear, but the former is increasing and the latter is decreasing.

Figure 4

CSP Beams

Beam Length (ft)	1	2	3	4	5	6	7	8
Number of Rods	3	7	11	15	19	23	27	31

Figure 5

CSP Staircase Frames

Number of Steps	1	2	3	4	5	6	7	8
Number of Rods	4	10	18	28	40	54	70	88

Exploring Data Patterns

People in many professions use data and mathematical reasoning to solve problems and make predictions. For example, engineers analyze data from laboratory tests to determine how much weight a bridge can hold. Market researchers use customer survey data to predict demand for new products. Stockbrokers use algebraic formulas to forecast how much their investments will earn over time.

In several previous *Connected Mathematics* units, you used tables, graphs, and equations to explore and describe relationships between variables. In this investigation, you will develop your skill in using these tools to organize data from an experiment, find patterns, and make predictions.

1.1 Testing Bridge Thickness

Many bridges are built with frames of steel beams. Steel is very strong, but any beam will bend or break if you put enough weight on it. The amount of weight a beam can support is related to its thickness, length, and design. To design a bridge, engineers need to understand these relationships.

Notes _____

_____

_____

_____

- How do you think the thickness of a beam is related to its strength? Do you think the relationship is linear?
- What other variables might affect the strength of a bridge?

Engineers often use scale models to test their designs. You can do your own experiments to discover mathematical patterns involved in building bridges.

Instructions for the Bridge-Thickness Experiment

Equipment:

- Two books of the same thickness
- A small paper cup
- About 50 pennies
- Several 11-inch-by-$4\frac{1}{4}$-inch strips of paper

Instructions:

- Start with one of the paper strips. Make a "bridge" by folding up 1 inch on each long side.

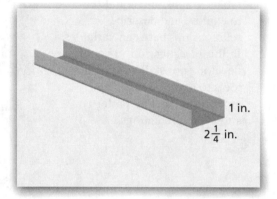

- Suspend the bridge between the books. The bridge should overlap each book by about 1 inch. Place the cup in the center of the bridge.

- Put pennies into the cup, one at a time, until the bridge collapses. Record the number of pennies you added to the cup. This number is the *breaking weight* of the bridge.

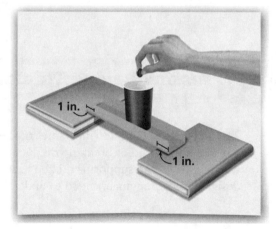

- Put two *new* strips of paper together to make a bridge of double thickness. Find the breaking weight for this bridge.

- Repeat this experiment to find the breaking weights of bridges made from three, four, and five strips of paper.

6   Thinking With Mathematical Models

Notes _____

_____

_____

_____

A. Conduct the bridge-thickness experiment to find breaking weights for bridges 1, 2, 3, 4, and 5 layers thick. Record your data in a table.

B. Make a graph of your (*bridge layers, breaking weight*) data.

C. Does the relationship between bridge thickness and breaking weight seem to be linear or nonlinear? How is this shown in the table and graph?

D. Suppose you could split layers of paper in half. What breaking weight would you predict for a bridge 2.5 layers thick? Explain.

E. 1. Predict the breaking weight for a bridge 6 layers thick. Explain your reasoning.

    2. Test your prediction. Explain why results from such tests might not exactly match predictions.

ACE Homework starts on page 12.

active math
online

For: Virtual Bridge Experiment
Visit: PHSchool.com
Web Code: apd-1101

STUDENT PAGE

Investigation 1 Exploring Data Patterns   **7**

STUDENT PAGE

Notes _____

_____

_____

_____

In the last problem, you tested paper bridges of various thicknesses. You found that thicker bridges are stronger than thinner bridges. In this problem, you will experiment with paper bridges of various lengths.

How do you think the length of a bridge is related to its strength?

Are longer bridges stronger or weaker than shorter bridges?

You can do an experiment to find out how the length and strength of a bridge are related.

Instructions for the Bridge-Length Experiment

Equipment:

- Two books of the same thickness
- A small paper cup
- About 50 pennies
- $4\frac{1}{4}$-inch-wide strips with lengths 4, 6, 8, 9, and 11 inches

Instructions:

- Make paper bridges from the strips. For each strip, fold up 1 inch on each of the $4\frac{1}{4}$-inch sides.

- Start with the 4-inch bridge. Suspend the bridge between the two books as you did before. The bridge should overlap each book by about 1 inch. Place the paper cup in the center of the bridge.

- Put pennies into the cup, one at a time, until the bridge collapses. Record the number of pennies you added to the cup. As in the first experiment, this number is the breaking weight of the bridge.

- Repeat the experiment to find breaking weights for the other bridges.

8 Thinking With Mathematical Models

Notes _____

_____

_____

_____

A. Conduct the bridge-length experiment to find breaking weights for bridges of lengths 4, 6, 8, 9, and 11 inches. Record your data in a table.

B. Make a graph of your data.

C. Describe the relationship between bridge length and breaking weight. How is that relationship shown by patterns in your table and graph?

D. Use your data to predict the breaking weights for bridges of lengths 3, 5, 10, and 12 inches. Explain how you made your predictions.

E. Compare your data from this experiment with the data from the bridge-thickness experiment. How is the relationship between bridge thickness and breaking weight similar to the relationship between bridge length and breaking weight? How is it different?

ACE **Homework starts on page 12.**

Did You Know ?

When designing a bridge, engineers need to consider the *load*, or the amount of weight, the bridge must support. The *dead load* is the weight of the bridge and fixed objects on the bridge. The *live load* is the weight of moving objects on the bridge.

On many city bridges in Europe— such as the famous Ponte Vecchio in Florence, Italy—dead load is very high because tollbooths, apartments, and shops are built right onto the bridge surface. Local ordinances can limit the amount of automobile and rail traffic on a bridge to help control live load.

Investigation 1 Exploring Data Patterns   **9**

Notes _____

_____

_____

_____

1.3 Custom Construction Parts

Suppose a company called Custom Steel Products (CSP for short) provides construction materials to builders. CSP makes beams and staircase frames by attaching 1-foot-long steel rods in the following patterns. CSP will make these materials in any size a builder needs.

CSP Beams

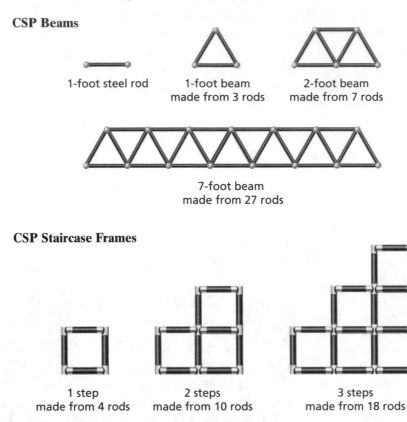

1-foot steel rod

1-foot beam
made from 3 rods

2-foot beam
made from 7 rods

7-foot beam
made from 27 rods

CSP Staircase Frames

1 step
made from 4 rods

2 steps
made from 10 rods

3 steps
made from 18 rods

The manager at CSP needs to know the number of rods required for each design in any size a customer might order. To figure this out, she decides to study a few simple cases. She hopes to find *trends,* or patterns, she can extend to other cases.

Notes _____

_____

_____

_____

Problem 1.3 **Extending Patterns**

A. 1. Copy and complete the table below to show the number of rods in beams of different lengths. **Hint:** Make drawings of the beams.

CSP Beams

Beam Length (ft)	1	2	3	4	5	6	7	8
Number of Rods	3	7	■	■	■	■	27	■

2. Make a graph of the data in your table.

3. Describe the pattern of change in the number of rods as the beam length increases.

4. How is the pattern you described shown in the table? How is it shown in the graph?

5. How many steel rods are in a beam of length 50 feet? Explain.

B. 1. Copy and complete the table below to show the number of rods in staircase frames with different numbers of steps. **Hint:** Make drawings of the staircase frames.

CSP Staircase Frames

Number of Steps	1	2	3	4	5	6	7	8
Number of Rods	4	10	18	■	■	■	■	■

2. Make a graph of the data in your table.

3. Describe the pattern of change in the number of rods as the number of steps increases.

4. How is the pattern you described shown in the table? How is it shown in the graph?

5. How many steel rods are in a staircase frame with 12 steps?

C. How is the pattern of change in Question A similar to the pattern in Question B? How is it different? Explain how the similarities and differences are shown in the tables and graphs.

D. Compare the patterns of change in this problem with the patterns of change in Problems 1.1 and 1.2. Describe any similarities and differences you find.

ACE Homework starts on page 12.

Notes _____

_____

_____

_____

Applications

1. A group of students conducts the bridge-thickness experiment with construction paper. Their results are shown in this table.

Bridge-Thickness Experiment

Thickness (layers)	1	2	3	4	5	6
Breaking Weight (pennies)	12	20	29	42	52	61

a. Make a graph of the (*thickness, breaking weight*) data. Describe the relationship between thickness and breaking weight.

b. Suppose it is possible to use half-layers of construction paper. What breaking weight would you predict for a bridge 3.5 layers thick? Explain.

c. Predict the breaking weight for a construction-paper bridge 8 layers thick. Explain how you made your prediction.

2. The table shows the maximum weight a crane arm can lift at various distances from its cab. (See the diagram below.)

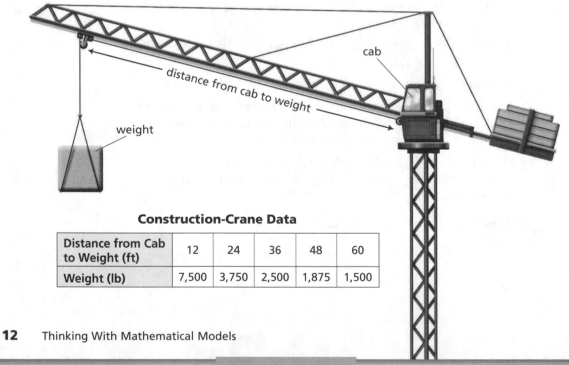

Construction-Crane Data

Distance from Cab to Weight (ft)	12	24	36	48	60
Weight (lb)	7,500	3,750	2,500	1,875	1,500

12 Thinking With Mathematical Models

Notes _____

_____

_____

_____

a. Describe the relationship between distance and weight for the crane.

b. Make a graph of the (*distance, weight*) data. Explain how the graph's shape shows the relationship you described in part (a).

c. Estimate the weight the crane can lift at distances of 18 feet, 30 feet, and 72 feet from the cab.

d. How, if at all, is the crane data similar to the data from the bridge experiments in Problems 1.1 and 1.2?

3. A beam or staircase frame from CSP costs $2.25 for each rod, plus $50 for shipping and handling.

a. Refer to your data for Question A of Problem 1.3. Copy and complete the following table to show the costs for beams of different lengths.

Costs of CSP Beams

Beam Length (ft)	1	2	3	4	5	6	7	8
Number of Rods	3	7	■	■	■	■	27	■
Cost of Beam	■	■	■	■	■	■	■	■

b. Make a graph of the (*beam length, cost*) data.

c. Describe the relationship between beam length and cost.

d. Refer to your data for Question B of Problem 1.3. Copy and complete the following table to show the costs for staircase frames with different numbers of steps.

Costs of CSP Staircase Frames

Number of Steps	1	2	3	4	5	6	7	8
Number of Rods	4	10	18	■	■	■	■	■
Cost of Frame	■	■	■	■	■	■	■	■

e. Make a graph of the (*number of steps, cost*) data.

f. Describe the relationship between the number of steps and the cost.

Notes _____

4. Parts (a)–(f) refer to relationships you have studied in this investigation. Tell whether each relationship is linear.

   a. the relationship between beam length and cost (ACE Exercise 3)

   b. the relationship between the number of steps in a staircase frame and the cost (ACE Exercise 3)

   c. the relationship between bridge thickness and strength (Problem 1.1)

   d. the relationship between bridge length and strength (Problem 1.2)

   e. the relationship between beam length and the number of rods (Problem 1.3)

   f. the relationship between the number of steps in a staircase frame and the number of rods (Problem 1.3)

   g. Compare the patterns of change for all the nonlinear relationships in parts (a)–(f).

Homework Help Online
PHSchool.com
For: Help with Exercise 4
Web Code: ape-1104

5. In many athletic competitions, medals are awarded to top athletes. The medals are often awarded in ceremonies with medal winners standing on special platforms. The sketches show how to make platforms by stacking boxes.

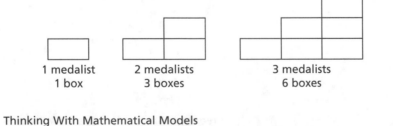

1 medalist
1 box

2 medalists
3 boxes

3 medalists
6 boxes

Notes _____

_____

_____

_____

a. Copy and complete the table below.

Medal Platforms

Number of Medalists	1	2	3	4	5	6	7	8
Number of Boxes	1	3	6	■	■	■	■	■

b. Make a graph of the (*number of medalists, number of boxes*) data.

c. Describe the pattern of change shown in the table and graph.

d. Each box is 1 foot high and 2 feet wide. A red carpet starts 10 feet from the base of the platform, and covers all the risers and steps.

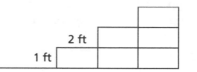

Copy and complete the table below.

Carpet for Platforms

Number of Steps	1	2	3	4	5	6	7	8
Carpet Length (ft)	■	■	■	■	■	■	■	■

e. Make a graph of the (*number of steps, carpet length*) data.

f. Describe the pattern of change in the carpet length as the number of steps increases. Compare this pattern with the pattern in the (*number of medalists, number of boxes*) data.

6. CSP also sells ladder bridges made from 1-foot steel rods arranged to form a row of squares. Below is a 6-foot ladder bridge.

6-foot ladder bridge made from 19 rods

a. Make a table and a graph showing how the number of rods in a ladder bridge is related to length of the bridge.

b. Compare the pattern of change for the ladder bridges with those for the beams and staircase frames in Problem 1.3.

Investigation 1 Exploring Data Patterns **15**

Notes _____

_____

_____

_____

Connections

A survey of one class at Pioneer Middle School finds that
20 out of 30 students would spend $8 for a school T-shirt.
Use this information for Exercises 7 and 8.

7. **Multiple Choice** Suppose there are 600 students in the
school. Based on the survey, how many students do you
predict would spend $8 for a school T-shirt?

   A. 20   **B.** 200

   C. 300   **D.** 400

8. **Multiple Choice** Suppose there are 450 students in the
school. Based on the survey, how many students do you
predict would spend $8 for a school T-shirt?

   F. 20   **G.** 200

   H. 300   **J.** 400

9. Below is a drawing of a rectangle with an area of
   300 square feet.

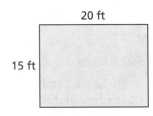

   a. Make drawings of at least three other rectangles with an area
   of 300 square feet.

   b. What is the width of a rectangle with an area of 300 square feet if
   its length is 1 foot? If its length is 2 feet? If its length is 3 feet?

   c. What is the width of a rectangle with an area of 300 square feet
   and a length of L feet?

   d. How does the width of a rectangle change if the length increases,
   but the area remains 300 square feet?

   e. Make a graph of (*width, length*) pairs for a rectangle that give an
   area of 300 square feet. Explain how your graph illustrates your
   answer for part (d).

Notes _____

_____

_____

_____

10. **a.** The rectangle pictured in Exercise 9 has a perimeter of 70 feet. Make drawings of at least three other rectangles with a perimeter of 70 feet.

   b. What is the width of a rectangle with a perimeter of 70 feet if its length is 1 foot? 2 feet? L feet?

   c. What is the width of a rectangle with a perimeter of 70 feet if its length is $\frac{1}{2}$ foot? $\frac{3}{2}$ feet?

   d. Give the dimensions of rectangles with perimeters of 70 feet and length-to-width ratios of 3 to 4, 4 to 5, and 1 to 1.

   e. Suppose the length of a rectangle increases, but the perimeter remains at 70 feet. How does the width change?

   f. Make a graph of (*width, length*) pairs that give a perimeter of 70 feet. How does your graph illustrate your answer for part (e)?

11. The 24 students in Ms. Cleary's homeroom are surveyed. They are asked which of several prices they would pay for a ticket to the school fashion show. The results are shown in this table.

Ticket-Price Survey

Ticket Price	$1.00	$1.50	$2.00	$2.50	$3.00	$3.50	$4.00	$4.50
Probable Sales	20	20	18	15	12	10	8	7

   a. There are 480 students in the school. Use the data from Ms. Cleary's class to predict ticket sales for the entire school for each price.

   b. Use your results from part (a). For each price, find the school's projected income from ticket sales.

   c. Which price should the school charge if it wants to earn the maximum possible income?

Middletown High School Presents:
The Spring Fashion Show
Featuring
★ **Mathematical Models** ★

Friday, May 23, at 7:00 PM
Middletown High School Auditorium

ADMIT ONE

Investigation 1 Exploring Data Patterns **17**

Notes _____

_____

_____

_____

Tell which graph matches the equation or the set of criteria.

12. $y = 3x + 1$ **13.** $y = -2x + 2$

14. $y = x - 3$ **15.** y-intercept $= 1$; slope $= \frac{1}{2}$

Graph A

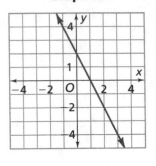

Graph B

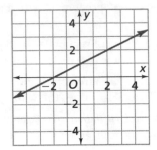

Graph C

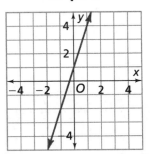

Graph D

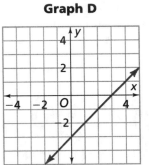

Within each equation, the pouches shown contain the same number of coins. Find the number of coins in each pouch. Explain your method.

16.

17.

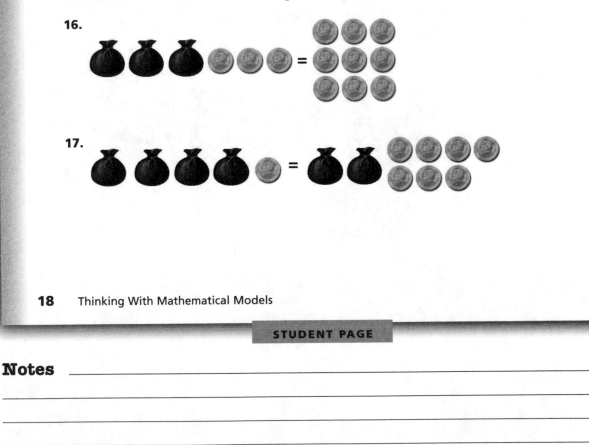

Notes _____

_____

_____

_____

18. Refer to Exercises 16 and 17.

    a. For each exercise, write an equation to represent the situation. Let x represent the number of coins in a pouch.

    b. Solve each equation. Explain the steps in your solutions.

    c. Compare your strategies with those you used in Exercises 16 and 17.

Solve each equation for x.

Go Online
PHSchool.com
For: Multiple-Choice Skills Practice
Web Code: apa-1154

19. $3x + 4 = 10$ **20.** $6x + 3 = 4x + 11$

21. $6x - 3 = 11$ **22.** $-3x + 5 = 7$

23. $4x - \frac{1}{2} = 8$ **24.** $\frac{x}{2} - 4 = -5$

25. $3x + 3 = -2x - 12$ **26.** $\frac{x}{4} - 4 = \frac{3x}{4} - 6$

For Exercises 27–29, tell whether the statement is *true* or *false*. Explain your reasoning.

27. $6(12 - 5) > 50$ **28.** $3 \cdot 5 - 4 > 6$ **29.** $10 - 5 \cdot 4 > 0$

30. You will need two sheets of 8.5- by 11-inch paper and some scrap paper.

    a. Roll one sheet of paper to make a cylinder 11 inches high. Overlap the edges very slightly and tape them together. Make bases for the cylinder by tracing the circles on the ends of the cylinder, cutting out the tracings, and taping them in place.

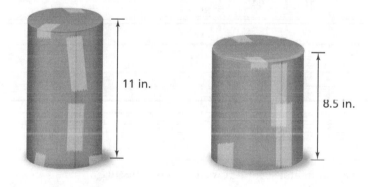

    b. Roll the other sheet of paper to make a cylinder 8.5 inches high. Make bases as you did in part (a).

    c. Do the cylinders appear to have the same surface area (including the bases)? If not, which has the greater surface area?

    d. Suppose you start with two identical rectangular sheets of paper which are *not* 8.5 by 11 inches. You make two cylinders as you did before. Which cylinder will have the greater surface area, the taller cylinder or the shorter one? How do you know?

Investigation 1 Exploring Data Patterns   **19**

Notes _____

_____

_____

_____

31. The volume of the cone in the drawing at right is $\frac{1}{3}(28)\pi$. What are some possible radius and height measurements for the cone?

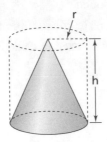

Extensions

32. Study the patterns in this table. Note that the numbers in the x column may not be consecutive after $x = 6$.

x	p	q	y	z
1	1	1	2	1
2	4	8	4	$\frac{1}{2}$
3	9	27	8	$\frac{1}{3}$
4	16	64	16	$\frac{1}{4}$
5	25	125	32	$\frac{1}{5}$
6	■	■	■	■
■	■	■	1,024	■
■	■	■	2,048	■
■	■	1,728	■	■
n	■	■	■	■

a. Use the patterns in the first several rows to find the missing values.

b. Are any of the patterns linear? Explain.

Notes _____

_____

_____

_____

33. The table gives data for a group of middle school students.

Data for Middle School Students

Student	Name Length	Height (cm)	Foot Length (cm)
Thomas Petes	11	126	23
Michelle Hughes	14	117	21
Shoshana White	13	112	17
Deborah Locke	12	127	21
Tonya Stewart	12	172	32
Richard Mudd	11	135	22
Tony Tung	8	130	20
Janice Vick	10	134	21
Bobby King	9	156	29
Kathleen Boylan	14	164	28

a. Make a graph of the (*name length, height*) data, a graph of the (*name length, foot length*) data, and a graph of the (*height, foot length*) data.

b. Look at the graphs you made in part (a). Which seem to show linear relationships? Explain.

c. Estimate the average height-to-foot-length ratio. That is, how many "feet" tall is the typical student in the table?

d. Which student has the greatest height-to-foot-length ratio? Which student has the least height-to-foot-length ratio?

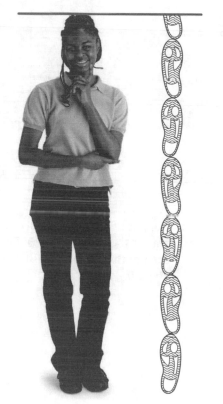

Investigation 1 Exploring Data Patterns   **21**

Notes _____

_____

_____

_____

34. A staircase is a prism. This is easier to see if the staircase is viewed from a different perspective. In the prism below, the small squares on the top each have an area of 1 square unit.

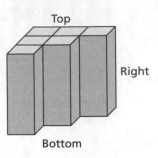

Top

Right

Bottom

a. Sketch the base of the prism. What is the area of the base?

b. Rashid is trying to draw a *net* (flat pattern) that will fold up to form the staircase prism. Below is the start of his drawing. Finish Rashid's drawing and give the surface area of the entire staircase.
Hint: You may want to draw your net on grid paper and then cut it out and fold it to check.

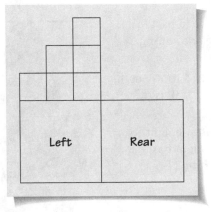

Left   Rear

c. Suppose the prism had six stairs instead of three. Assume each stair is the same width as those in the prism above. Is the surface area of this six-stair prism twice that of the three-stair prism? Explain.

Notes _____

_____

_____

_____

Mathematical Reflections 1

In this investigation, you used tables and graphs to represent relationships between variables and to make predictions. These questions will help you summarize what you have learned.

Think about your answers to these questions. Discuss your ideas with other students and your teacher. Then write a summary of your findings in your notebook.

You can represent a relationship between variables with a table, a graph, or a description in words.

1. What are the advantages and disadvantages of each representation for finding patterns and making predictions?

2. How can you decide from a table whether a relationship is linear?

3. How can you decide from a graph whether a relationship is linear?

Notes _____

_____

_____

_____

Answers

Applications **Connections** **Extensions**

Investigation 1

ACE Assignment Choices

Problem 1.1
Core 1
Other *Connections* 7–15

Problem 1.2
Core 2
Other *Connections* 16–22; unassigned choices from previous problems

Problem 1.3
Core 3–6
Other *Connections* 23–31; *Extensions* 32–34; unassigned choices from previous problems

Adapted For suggestions about adapting ACE exercises, see the *CMP Special Needs Handbook*.
Connecting to Prior Units 7, 8, 11: *Comparing and Scaling*; 9: *Covering and Surrounding*; 10: *Covering and Surrounding, Bits and Pieces II, Comparing and Scaling*; 12–26: *Moving Straight Ahead*; 27–29: *Accentuate the Negative*; 30, 31: *Filling and Wrapping*

Applications

1. a.

Bridge-Thickness Experiment

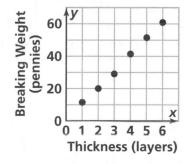

The data are very close to linear. Each time the class adds a layer, the bridge can hold approximately ten more pennies.

b. Possible answer: 35 pennies. The breaking weight is about 10 pennies per layer. So, for 3.5 layers, it would be 35.

c. Possible answer: 80. The breaking weight is about 10 pennies per layer. So, for 8 layers, it would be about 80.

2. a. As distance increases, weight decreases. The decrease is sharper at shorter distances. (The product of distance and weight is always 90,000.)

b. The graph shows that as distance increases, weight decreases—sharply at first, and then more gradually.

Crane Lifting Capacity

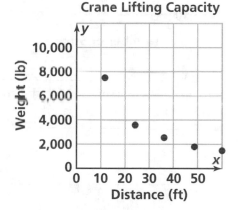

c. ≈ 5,000 lb; ≈ 3,000 lb; ≈ 1,250 lb

d. The graph's shape is similar to that for the bridge-length experiment because the values of the dependent variable decrease at a decreasing rate. (**Note:** You may want to revisit this problem after Problem 3.2 so that students can check their estimates.)

3. a. (Figure 6)

Figure 6

Costs of CSP Beams

Beam Length (ft)	1	2	3	4	5	6	7	8
Number of Rods	3	7	11	15	19	23	27	31
Cost of Beam	$56.75	$65.75	$74.75	$83.75	$92.75	$101.75	$110.75	$119.75

b.

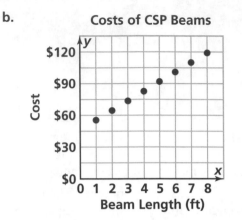

Costs of CSP Beams

c. This is a linear relationship. As beam length increases by 1 unit, cost increases by $9.

d. (Figure 7)

e.

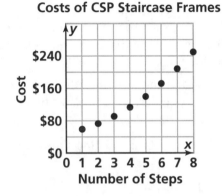

Costs of CSP Staircase Frames

f. This is not a linear relationship. As the number of steps increases by 1, the cost increases at an increasing rate.

4. a. linear   **b.** not linear
  c. linear   **d.** not linear
  e. linear   **f.** nonlinear
  g. The relationships in parts (b) and (f) are increasing, but at different rates. The relationship in part (d) is decreasing.

5. a. (Figure 8)

  b.

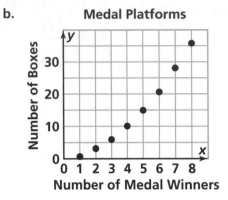

Medal Platforms

  c. This is not a linear relationship. In the table, when we add the second medal winner, we add 2 boxes. When we add a third medal winner, we add 3 more boxes. To add a 29th medal winner, we add 29 boxes to a 28-step platform. The change is increasing at each step. We see this in the graph because the graph rises more and more sharply as we move left to right along the x-axis.

Figure 7

Costs of CSP Staircase Frames

Number of Steps	1	2	3	4	5	6	7	8
Number of Rods	4	10	18	28	40	54	70	88
Cost of Frame	$59	$72.50	$90.50	$113	$140	$171.50	$207.50	$248

Figure 8

Medal Platforms

Number of Medalists	1	2	3	4	5	6	7	8
Number of Boxes	1	3	6	10	15	21	28	36

d. (Figure 9)

e.

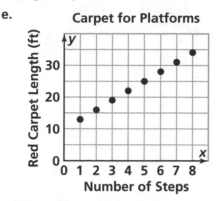

Carpet for Platforms

f. The pattern in the data illustrates a linear relationship because, with every new step, the length of the red carpet increases by exactly 3 feet. This constant rate of change is different than the pattern in the number of boxes, which has an increasing rate of change.

6. a. (Figure 10)

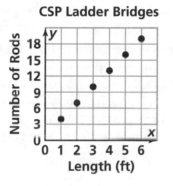

CSP Ladder Bridges

b. This is an increasing linear relationship like the relationship between beam length and number of rods. Although the relationship between number of steps and number of rods in a staircase frame is also increasing, it is not linear.

Connections

7. D ($\frac{2}{3}$ of 600)

8. H ($\frac{2}{3}$ of 450)

9. a. Possible rectangles:

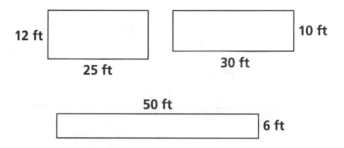

b. 300 feet; 150 feet; 100 feet

c. $\frac{300}{L}$ feet (Note: Some students may not be able to use symbols to describe this relationship. They will work more with the relationship between area, length, and width in Investigation 3.)

d. The width decreases, but not linearly.

Figure 9

Carpet for Platforms

Number of Steps	1	2	3	4	5	6	7	8
Carpet Length (ft)	13	16	19	22	25	28	31	34

Figure 10

CSP Ladder Bridges

Bridge Length (ft)	1	2	3	4	5	6
Number of Rods	4	7	10	13	16	19

e.

Rectangles With an Area of 300 ft²

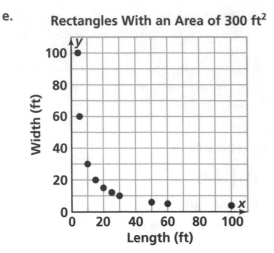

The graph decreases very sharply at first and then more gradually.

10. a.

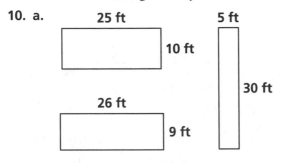

b. 34 ft; 33 ft; 35 − L ft, or 0.5(70 − 2L) ft

c. 34.5 feet, 33.5 feet

d. 15 ft by 20 ft; about 15.4 ft by 19.25 ft; 17.5 ft by 17.5 ft

e. It decreases linearly.

f.

Rectangles With a Perimeter of 70 ft

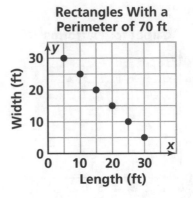

We see a linear decrease in the graph.

11. a. See the "Probable Sales" row of Figure 11.

b. See the "Income" row of Figure 11.

c. $2.50

12. Graph C

13. Graph A

14. Graph D

15. Graph B

16. 2 coins; possible method: Take 3 coins from each side to get 3 pouches equals 6 coins. Because each pouch contains the same number of coins, there must be 2 coins in each pouch.

17. 3 coins; possible method: Take 1 coin from each side to get 4 pouches equals 2 pouches and 6 coins. Now take 2 pouches from each side to get 2 pouches equals 6 coins. Because each pouch contains the same number of coins, there must be 3 coins in each pouch.

Figure 11

Predicted Ticket Sales for Whole School

Ticket Price	$1.00	$1.50	$2.00	$2.50	$3.00	$3.50	$4.00	$4.50
Probable Sales	400	400	360	300	240	200	160	140
Income	$400	$600	$720	$750	$720	$700	$640	$630

18. a. $3x + 3 = 9$ and $4x + 1 = 2x + 7$

b. Possible solution for $3x + 3 = 9$:

$$3x + 3 = 9$$
$$3x = 6 \quad \text{Subtract 3 from each side.}$$
$$x = 2 \quad \text{Divide each side by 3.}$$

Possible solution for $4x + 1 = 2x + 7$:

$$4x + 1 = 2x + 7$$
$$4x = 2x + 6 \quad \text{Subtract 1 from each side.}$$
$$2x = 6 \quad \text{Subtract } 2x \text{ from each side.}$$
$$x = 3 \quad \text{Divide both sides by 2.}$$

c. Possible answer: The strategies were the same, but in part (b), symbols were used instead of objects.

19. $x = 2$

20. $x = 4$

21. $x = \frac{14}{6}$ or an equivalent form

22. $x = \frac{-2}{3}$

23. $x = 2\frac{1}{8}$ or $x = 2.125$

24. $x = -2$

25. $x = -3$

26. $x = 4$

27. False, because $42 < 50$

28. True, because $11 > 6$

29. False, because $-10 < 0$

30. a–c. The "wrap" part of the cylinder has the same area (8.5×11) for each cylinder, but the circular bases are larger for the cylinder with the 8.5-inch height.

d. The shorter cylinder. The base area depends on the radius. If the smaller dimension of the paper is used for the height of the cylinder, then the base area will have a larger radius.

31. Answers will vary. The only criterion is that $r^2h = 28$. Possible answers: $r = 2, h = 7$; $r = \sqrt{7}, h = 4; r = \sqrt{8}, h = 3.5$.

Extensions

32. a.

x	p	q	y	z
1	1	1	2	1
2	4	8	4	$\frac{1}{2}$
3	9	27	8	$\frac{1}{3}$
4	16	64	16	$\frac{1}{4}$
5	25	125	32	$\frac{1}{5}$
6	36	216	64	$\frac{1}{6}$
10	100	1,000	1,024	$\frac{1}{10}$
11	121	1,331	2,048	$\frac{1}{11}$
12	144	1,728	4,096	$\frac{1}{12}$
n	n^2	n^3	2^n	$\frac{1}{n}$

b. None of the patterns are linear because a constant change in x does not yield a constant change in y.

33. a.

Name Length vs. Height

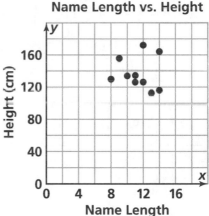

Name Length vs. Foot Length

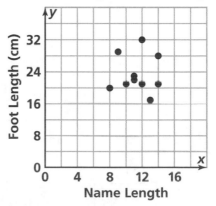

Height vs. Foot Length

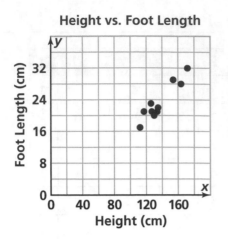

b. Only the (*height, foot length*) graph looks linear.

c. Approximately 6 : 1; The average student is 6 "feet" tall.

d. Shoshana White; Tonya Stewart

34. a. Orientation of base will vary; 6 sq. units

b.

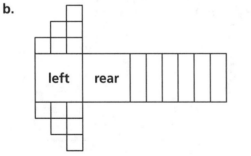

Figure 12

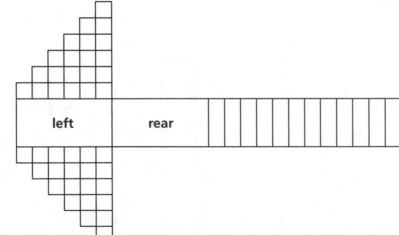

Surface area = 6 (top) + 6 (bottom) + 9 (left) + 9 (rear) + (3 + 3) + (3 + 3) + (3 + 3) = 48 sq. units.

c. New surface area: 21 (top) + 21 (bottom) + 18 (left) + 18 (rear) + (3 + 3) + (3 + 3) + (3 + 3) + (3 + 3) + (3 + 3) + (3 + 3) = 114 sq. units. The top and bottom areas more than doubled. The left and rear areas exactly doubled (but they are no longer squares). The "stair" area doubles. So the total area is more than twice the original. A flat pattern is shown in Figure 12.

Possible Answers to Mathematical Reflections

1. One advantage to a graph is that it gives a visual representation of the situation. A disadvantage is that a graph can be difficult to read for precise answers. An advantage of words is that they can communicate a situation easily without much effort on the part of the communicator, but sometimes words are not very precise. Some situations are just too complicated to explain easily in words. Tables give you precise information about certain coordinates, but they often leave you guessing about the information between the given coordinates.

2. If constant change in the independent variable in the table yields constant change in the dependent variable, then the relationship is linear.

3. If a graph is a straight line, the relationship is linear.

Investigation 2 — Linear Models and Equations

Mathematical and Problem-Solving Goals

- Fit a line to data that show a linear trend
- Use mathematical models to answer questions about linear relationships
- Practice effective strategies for writing linear equations from verbal, numerical, or graphical information
- Develop skill in solving linear equations with approximation and exact reasoning methods
- Write inequalities to represent "at most" situations
- Use equations to represent questions about problem situations and interpret the solutions in the context of the problem

Mathematics Background

For background on mathematical modeling, see page 5.

Summary of Problems

Problem 2.1 Linear Models

Students are introduced to *mathematical models* for data sets. They find linear models—both graphs and equations—for data sets, and use the models to make predictions.

Problem 2.2 Equations for Linear Relationships

Students review and extend their understanding and skill in writing linear equations to match conditions expressed in words, tables, and graphs.

Problem 2.3 Solving Linear Equations

Students use tables and graphs to estimate solutions to linear equations and inequalities and use symbolic reasoning to find exact solutions.

Problem 2.4 Intersecting Linear Models

Students use their knowledge about linear models, equations, and inequalities to reason about related sets of linear data.

	Suggested Pacing	Materials for Students	Materials for Teachers	ACE Assignments
All	6 days	Calculators, grid paper, blank transparencies and transparency markers (optional); chart paper and markers (optional); student notebooks	Blank transparencies and transparency markers (optional), chart paper and markers (optional)	
2.1	$1\frac{1}{2}$ days	Graphing calculators (optional), Labsheet 2ACE Exercise 3	Strand of uncooked spaghetti or another thin, straight object; Transparencies 2.1A and 2.1B	1, 2, 3, 35, 36
2.2	$1\frac{1}{2}$ days	Graphing calculators (optional)	Transparencies 2.2A and 2.2B	4–19, 37–42, 57–63
2.3	1 day		Transparency 2.3	20–24, 43
2.4	$1\frac{1}{2}$ days	Graphing calculators (optional), transparent grids (optional)		25–34, 44–56
MR	$\frac{1}{2}$ day			

Goals

- Fit a line to data that show a linear trend

- Write an equation for a line based on a graph of the line

- Use mathematical models to answer questions about linear relationships

In this problem, students think about data using linear models and begin to understand the value and power of mathematical models. This problem focuses on linear models. Methods for finding an equation of a line were first introduced in *Moving Straight Ahead*. In this problem, we assume that students are familiar with the concepts of slope and *y*-intercept and have had experience writing equations for lines given the slope and the *y*-intercept. They review and extend those concepts and skills as they find equations for lines that model sets of data.

Launch

Introduce the context of the bridge-painting company bidding on a project. You might begin by showing students the graph without the modeling line drawn in, which appears on the top half of Transparency 2.1A.

Suggested Question

- *Do you see a pattern in these data?* (They are almost linear.)

Explain that because the data are approximately linear, we can use a line to model the trend.

Have a discussion about where the line should go to approximate the data. You might use a strand of uncooked spaghetti to represent the line on the overhead projector. Students can give you feedback as you move the line to try to find a good fit.

Some students draw modeling lines by joining the first and last points. Others try to place the line so there are an equal number of points above and below, rather than focusing on the overall trend. In this situation, those methods could produce quite reasonable models. However, as general strategies, they have limitations.

Suggested Questions You might ask questions like these and draw examples to deepen students' insights about good modeling lines:

- *Do you think connecting the first and last points in a data set will always give a line that fits the pattern?* (No; the line might not come close to several of the other points.)

- *Can you think of a situation in which that line would not be a good representative of the overall relationship?* (Possible answer: a situation in which the first or last data point does not fit the pattern in the rest of the data.)

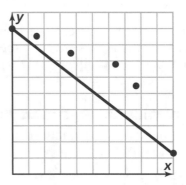

- *Will any line that has an equal number of points above and below be a good model?* (No; it is most important that the line fit the pattern of points. If the points on one or both sides are far from the line, then the line is not a good model.)

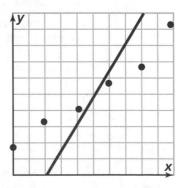

When the class has agreed on a line, draw it on the transparency.

- *How can we find the equation for our line?* (Students should discuss finding the slope and *y*-intercept to write an equation in the form $y = mx + b$.)

- *Can we use our line or equation to predict the costs for other bridges? How?* (Find the point on the line corresponding to the length of the bridge. The *y*-coordinate of the point is the cost. Or, substitute the length for *x* in the equation $y = mx + b$ and find the value of *y*.)

Introduce the term *mathematical model* to describe the relationship of the line to the data pattern. You might ask students to describe other situations in which the word "model" is used and to explain what the word means in those situations. For example, a model train or model airplane is a toy that is like a real train or plane in some respects. Seeing a model train or plane would help someone to understand what the real object is like. Similarly, a mathematical model helps people understand the pattern in a set of data.

Have students compare the linear model the class made with the one in the student text. The graph is reproduced on the bottom half of Transparency 2.1A.

Suggested Questions

- *Does the linear model in the book have the same slope as our model? Does it have the same y-intercept?* (The models should be close to the same, but probably will not be exactly the same.)

- *How would predictions made from the two models differ?* (Possible answer: For long bridges, beyond the range of the graph, the costs predicted by the models might be very different.)

Ask students to think individually about the Getting Ready questions for a few minutes. Then pair them with partners to share their thinking. Finally, discuss the questions as a class.

As you discuss the Getting Ready questions, try to focus on reviewing strategies, rather than on specific calculations. Students are asked to calculate specific values in the problem.

Note to the Teacher The linear models shown are approximations, but they are not necessarily "lines of best fit." A line of best fit must be tested with a correlation. Our intent is to reasonably model the data to make good predictions.

Suggested Questions

- *How do you think the cost estimators decided where to draw the line?* (Answers will vary. It is important that students discuss the overall pattern in the data, rather than focusing on a strategy that may not work for other situations, such as having equal numbers of points above and below the line.)

- *Do you think the line is a reasonable model for these data?* (Yes; it is very close to the data and shows the overall trend.)

- *What information does the model give that the four points alone do not?* [The model suggests other (*length, cost*) pairs that have a relationship similar to the known data.]

- *What questions could you answer using the model?* (You could find the approximate cost of painting a bridge with any length between 0 and 500 feet. You could find the length of a bridge that could be painted for a given cost, up to about $80,000. You could find the fixed cost that applies to any bridge, regardless of length. This is the *y*-intercept, which is about $5,000. You could find the rate at which the painting cost increases as the bridge length increases. This is the slope of the modeling line, which is about $150 per foot.)

- *What information do you need to write an equation for the line?* (You need the slope and *y*-intercept, or you need the coordinates of at least two points on the line so you can use them to find the slope and *y*-intercept.)

Explain to students that in Problem 2.1, they will find an equation to match the line and use that equation and the line to answer questions about the relationship between bridge length and painting cost. Then they will look at painting costs for a different type of bridge.

The class can work in pairs or groups of three. Summarize Question A when most students have completed it, and then have students move on to Question B.

Explore 2.1

As you observe students, keep an eye out to see whether they come up with an appropriate equation.

Suggested Questions Ask:

- *What does the slope mean in terms of bridge length and painting cost?* (It costs approximately $150 more for every 1-foot increase in bridge length.)

- *What does the* y-intercept *tell you about bridge length and painting cost?* (There is a fixed $5,000 cost, no matter how long the bridge is.)

When students use the model to answer questions, as in parts (2) and (3) of Question A, watch to see whether they use the graph to estimate the answers or whether they use the equation and symbolic reasoning to find the exact answers. For those who use only one strategy, ask if they could get their answers another way.

You might also ask students how they could use a graphing calculator to produce the graph of the equation model.

All of this work should give you good information about what students recall from *Moving Straight Ahead* in grade 7.

You do not need to stop to formally review the various strategies students might use. These strategies are reviewed in Problems 2.2 and 2.3.

When students work on Question B, look at the plot they produce from the data and probe to see how students choose where to draw a reasonable modeling line.

You might ask some groups to prepare transparencies of their work to share during the summary discussion.

Summarize 2.1

Summarize Question A, then have students do Question B to check their understanding. You could assign Question B as homework and summarize it the next day. It doesn't involve new skills; the questions are similar to those in Question A.

While discussing Question A, have students demonstrate finding the solutions both by using a graph to approximate the answer and by finding an exact solution with the equation.

Suggested Questions

- *Who used the line to find approximate answers for parts (2) and (3)? Show us how you found the answers.*

- *Who used the equation to find exact answers for parts (2) and (3)? Show us how you found the answers.*

You may want to discuss variations in their answers to Question B. Students probably will have found slightly different y-intercepts or slopes. Have students display their lines on a transparency and describe how they thought about the problem.

Suggested Questions Asking questions like these will help students focus on key issues:

- *What directions would you give someone to help him or her draw a mathematical model?* (Possible answer: Draw a line that is close to as many points as possible.)

- *Once you have drawn the line, how do you find the slope and* y-intercept? (Find the slope by choosing two points on the line and finding the ratio of rise to run. Find the y-intercept by estimating the coordinate of the point where the line crosses the y-axis.)

- *How do the slope and* y-intercept *help you find the equation for the line?* (The equation is $y = mx + b$, where m is the slope and b is the y-intercept.)

As you end the discussion, focus students on the purpose of linear models.

- *If you have to make predictions from a linear model, which is more helpful, the equation or the line?* (Opinions will vary, but students should mention that the equation can give exact answers, while the graph gives a nice picture of the relationship.)

Revisit the plot of the data from Problem 1.1. Have students create a linear model for the (*bridge thickness, breaking weight*) data they collected in the experiment.

- *What are the advantages of having a linear model for your data set, rather than just a set of individual data points?* (Possible answer: If you have a linear model, you can use it to predict data points that are not in the table or graph. Another advantage is that you can see a general pattern, and an equation can help communicate that pattern.)

2.1 Linear Models

Mathematical Goals

- Fit a line to data that show a linear trend
- Write an equation for a line based on a graph of the line
- Use mathematical models to answer questions about linear relationships

Launch

Discuss the information the bridge-painting company is using. Show students the graph without the modeling line.

- *Do you see a pattern in these data?*

You might use a piece of uncooked spaghetti to find a line that fits.

- *How can we find the equation for our line?*
- *Can we use our line or equation to predict the costs for other bridges?*

Introduce the term *mathematical model*. Compare the class's line with the one in the student edition (bottom of Transparency 2.1A).

- *Does the linear model in the book have the same slope as our model?*
- *Does it have the same y-intercept?*
- *How would predictions made from the two models differ?*

Have students discuss the Getting Ready questions.

Materials
- Transparencies 2.1A and 2.1B
- Piece of uncooked spaghetti or other thin, straight object
- Graphing calculators (optional)

Explore

- *What does the slope mean in terms of bridge length and painting cost?*
- *What does the y-intercept tell you about bridge length and painting cost?*

When students use the model to answer questions, as in parts (2) and (3) of Question A, watch to see whether they use the graph to estimate the answers or whether they use the equation and symbolic reasoning to find the exact answers. For those who use only one strategy, ask if they could get their answers another way.

For Question B, probe to see how students decided where to draw their lines.

Summarize

Summarize Question A, then have students do Question B.

- *Who used the line to find approximate answers for parts (2) and (3)? Show us how you found the answers.*
- *Who used the equation to find exact answers for parts (2) and (3)? Show us how you found the answers.*

Materials
- Student notebooks

Vocabulary
- mathematical model

continued on next page

continued

Discuss variations in the answers to Question B. Have students display their graphs and explain how they decided where to draw their lines.

- *What directions would you give someone to help him or her draw a mathematical model?*
- *Once you have drawn the line, how do you find the slope and y-intercept?*
- *How do the slope and y-intercept help you find the equation?*
- *If you have to make predictions from a linear model, which is more helpful, the equation or the line?*

Have students make a linear model for their data from Problem 1.1.

- *What are the advantages of having a linear model for your data set, rather than just a set of individual data points?*

ACE Assignment Guide for Problem 2.1

Differentiated Instruction
Solutions for All Learners

Core 1–3 (**Note**: A Labsheet is provided for use with ACE Exercise 3.)
Other *Connections* 35, 36

Adapted For suggestions about adapting ACE exercises, see the CMP *Special Needs Handbook.*
Connecting to Prior Units 35, 36: *Moving Straight Ahead*

Answers to Problem 2.1

A. 1. $y = 150x + 5000$. Using coordinates from the line, such as $(100, 20{,}000)$ and $(300, 50{,}000)$, the slope is the ratio of the vertical change to the horizontal change: $\frac{30{,}000}{200} = 150$. The y-intercept can be estimated from the graph as $(0, 5{,}000)$.

2. a. $31,250. Use the equation, $y = 150x + 5{,}000$, to get $150 \cdot 175 + 5000 = 31{,}250$. Or, estimate by looking on the line for the y-coordinate corresponding to an x-coordinate of 175.

  b. $47,000. Solution methods are similar to those described in part (a).

3. a. About 33 ft. Find the x-coordinate of the point that has a y-coordinate of 10,000. Or, to find the exact value, solve $10{,}000 = 150x + 5{,}000$. The solution is $x = 33\frac{1}{3}$ ft.

b. About 370 ft. Solution methods are similar to those described in part (a).

B. 1. Possible line:

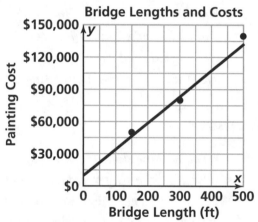

Bridge Lengths and Costs

2. Possible answer: $y = 250x + 8{,}000$

3. Answer should be close to $60,000. Students should either use the line to estimate the y-coordinate of the point with x-coordinate 200 or calculate $250(200) + 8{,}000$.

4. Answer should be close to 370 ft. Students may use the line to estimate the x-coordinate of the point with y-coordinate 100,000 or solve the equation $100{,}000 = 250x + 8{,}000$.

2.2 Equations for Linear Relationships

Goal

- Practice effective strategies for writing linear equations from verbal, numerical, or graphical information

The common setting for the questions of this problem is pricing schemes for self-operated car washes. Students are asked to write equations for linear relationships represented in tables, graphs, and verbal descriptions.

Launch 2.2

Introduce the context of self-service car washes.

Suggested Questions Talk with students about what variables they think are related to the price of washing a car.

- *What do you think self-service car wash owners consider when they decide how much to charge a customer?* (Possible answers: time the customer spends washing the car; the amount of water, soap, wax, and so on the customer uses)

Discuss the Getting Ready questions.

- *Sudzo Wash and Wax charges customers $0.75 per minute to wash a car. Write an equation that relates the total charge* c *to the amount of time* t *in minutes.* ($c = 0.75t$)

- *Pat's Power Wash charges $2.00 per car to cover the cost of cleaning supplies, plus $0.49 per minute for the use of water sprayers and vacuums. Write an equation for the total charge* c *for any car-wash time* t. ($c = 0.49t + 2$)

- *U-Wash-It charges $10 for each car. The business owners estimate that it costs them $0.60 per minute to provide soap, water, and vacuums for a car. Write an equation for the profit* p *U-Wash-It earns if a customer spends* t *minutes washing a car.* ($p = 10 - 0.60t$)

Record the equations on the board or overhead. As you discuss what the numbers and variables in each equation represent, record this information next to the equation.

- *Explain what the numbers and variables in each equation represent.* (The Sudzo and Pat's equations are similar. The coefficients, 0.75 and 0.49, represent the per-minute charge for washing a car. For U-Wash-It, the coefficient is the cost to the owner for each minute of use by a customer. The constant in the Pat's equation, 2, is an initial fee for using the wash. In the U-Wash-It equation, the constant is a flat fee per customer. The independent variable *t* represents the time the customer spends washing a car. The dependent variable for Sudzo and Pat's *c* represents the cost to the customer. The dependent variable for U-Wash-It *p* represents the profit the owners make.)

- *What questions can your equations help you answer?* (Possible answers: What is the charge at Sudzo if a customer uses the car wash for 5 minutes? How many minutes did a customer at Pat's wash her car if her charge was $4.94? When is the profit for U-Wash-It zero?)

Suggested Question Review some of the strategies students have for writing an equation.

- *What information do you need to write an equation that represents a linear relationship?* (the slope and the *y*-intercept)

- *What if all you are given is a table of data?* (Find the rate of change, which is the amount the dependent variable *y* changes as the independent variable *x* increases by 1. To find the *y*-intercept, or constant, work the values of the table back to when *x* = 0. Or, substitute values into $y = mx + b$ and solve for *b*.)

Students can work on the problem in pairs or groups of three.

Explore 2.2

Suggested Questions To help students monitor their own work on the problems, ask:

- *How can you check that the equations you write are correct?* (Possible answers: Substitute some of the given *x*-values into the equation to see if the correct *y*-values result. Use a graphing calculator to graph the equation, and then trace to the given *x*-values and compare the resulting *y*-values.)

INVESTIGATION 2

- *What information do you need to write an equation of a line?* (slope and y-intercept)

- *How are these values related to the equation* $y = mx + b$*?* (*m* is the slope and *b* is the y-intercept.)

- *How can you find the slope of a line?* (Given a graph or two points, find the ratio of the vertical change, rise, to the horizontal change, run. Given a table or a verbal description, find the rate of change.)

- *How can you find the* y*-intercept?* (Find the y-value when $x = 0$ on a graph or substitute values into $y = mx + b$ and solve for *b*.)

Summarize 2.2

Let students discuss their work. For Question F, have the class give an example for each part.

Suggested Questions At the end of the discussion, ask:

- *What two values are important when writing a linear equation?* (slope and y-intercept)

- *Which of these two is easier to find, in your opinion?* (Possible answer: It depends on the representation. On a graph, it is very easy to find at least an approximate y-intercept. In a table, if the x-value 0 is not included, it can take a lot of work to find the y-intercept, but we only need to do two subtractions and a division to find the slope.)

- *In an equation of the form,* $y = mx + b$, *what does each letter represent?* (*m* is the slope, or

rate of change; *b* is the y-intercept, or starting value; *x* is the independent variable; and *y* is the dependent variable.)

You can follow with these questions:

- *How can you find the slope if you are given the coordinates of two or more points on a graph?* (Start with two points and find the ratio of the vertical change, rise, to the horizontal change, run.)

- *How can you find the slope if you are given a table of* (x, y) *data values?* (Find the rate of change by looking at how the y-value increases for every increase of 1 in the x-value.)

- *How can you find the* y*-intercept from a table?* (Find the y-value when $x = 0$. If the x-value of 0 is not in the table, work the table back to $x = 0$.)

- *How can you find the* y*-intercept from a graph?* (Find the y-coordinate of the point where the line crosses the y-axis.)

Check for Understanding
- *Find an equation of the line through the points* (−3, 5) *and* (5, 25)*.* ($y = 2.5x + 12.5$)

- *Find an equation of the line parallel to* $y = 5 - 2x$ *that passes through the point* (3, 3)*.* [Any line with slope −2 is parallel to the line $y = 5 - 2x$. However, to pass through (3, 3), it must be $y = 9 - 2x$.]

2.2 Equations for Linear Relationships

At a Glance

PACING $1\frac{1}{2}$ days

Mathematical Goal

- Practice effective strategies for writing linear equations from verbal, numerical, or graphical information

Launch

Talk with students about what variables they think might be related to the price of washing a car at a self-service car wash.

Discuss the Getting Ready. As you discuss what the numbers and variables in each equation represent, record this information next to the equation.

- *What information do you need to write an equation that represents a linear relationship?*
- *What if all you are given is a table of data?*

Students can work on the problem in pairs or groups of three.

Materials
- Transparencies 2.2A and 2.2B

Explore

- *How can you check that the equations you write are correct?*
- *What information do you need to write an equation of a line?*
- *How are these values related to the equation* $y = mx + b$?
- *How can you find the slope of a line? How can you find the y-intercept?*

Summarize

Let students discuss their work. For Question F, have the class give an example for each part.

- *What two values are important when writing a linear equation? Which of these two is easier to find, in your opinion?*
- *In an equation of the form* $y = mx + b$, *what does each letter represent?*
- *How can you find the slope if you are given the coordinates of two or more points on a graph?*
- *How can you find the slope if you are given a table of (x, y) data values?*
- *How can you find the y-intercept from a table?*
- *How can you find the y-intercept from a graph?*

Materials
- Student notebooks
- Graphing calculators (optional)

Check for Understanding

- *Find an equation of the line through the points (−3, 5) and (5, 25).*
- *Find an equation of the line parallel to* $y = 5 - 2x$ *that passes through the point (3, 3).*

ACE Assignment Guide for Problem 2.2

Differentiated Instruction
Solutions for All Learners

Core 5–17
Other *Applications* 4, 18, 19; *Connections* 37–42, *Extensions* 57–63; unassigned choices from previous problems

Adapted For suggestions about adapting ACE Exercise 3, see the CMP *Special Needs Handbook.*

Answers to Problem 2.2

A. 1. For each 5-minute change in time, the charge increases by $5. Because the rate of change is constant, the relationship is linear.

2. The slope is 1 and the *y*-intercept is 3.

3. $c = t + 3$

B. $c = \frac{1}{3}t + 4$, where *t* is time used in minutes and *c* is the charge in dollars. The slope is $\frac{1}{3}$. It tells you the increase in charge for each additional minute of time. The 4 is the *y*-intercept, or starting value. It is a fixed charge customers pay.

C. 1. (10, 7) and (20, 12)

2. The slope is $\frac{1}{2}$, and the *y*-intercept is 2.

3. $c = \frac{1}{2}t + 2$

D. $y = -3x + 15$

E. $y = 2x - 3$

F. 1. Possible answer: Decide what the independent and dependent variables are. To find the value of *m*, look for a rate of increase or decrease. Sometimes the *b* value is given in words as a starting value. If it is not, use the rate of change to work backward to find what the value of the dependent variable would be when the independent variable is 0.

2. Possible answer: Find how much the *y*-value changes for every increase of 1 in the *x*-value. This rate of change can be determined by finding the ratio of the difference in two *y*-values to the difference in the corresponding two *x*-values, or $m = \frac{y_2 - y_1}{x_2 - x_1}$. The *y*-intercept can be found by working backward from given points to the point (0, _?_) using slope, or rate of change, information. Or, once *m* is known, substitute given values of *x* and *y* into the equation $y = mx + b$ and solve to find *b*.

3. Possible answer: Find the coordinates of two points the line passes through and proceed as described in the answer to part (2) to find the slope. Look for the coordinates of the *y*-intercept to find *b*.

2.3 Solving Linear Equations

Goals

- Develop skill in solving linear equations with approximation and exact reasoning methods

- Write inequalities to represent "at most" situations

Students learned methods for solving linear equations in *Moving Straight Ahead*. However, many students will benefit from a review of these methods. This section begins by posing questions in a Getting Ready that can be answered by solving linear equations. These questions provide you with an opportunity to assess students' understanding of solving equations and inequalities.

Note to the Teacher At this point, we expect students to use informal methods to solve inequalities. Students will learn formal methods in the unit *The Shapes of Algebra*.

Launch 2.3

On the board or overhead, write $c = 0.15t + 2.50$. Explain to students that c is the charge, in dollars, for renting a canoe for t minutes from Sandy's Boat House.

Suggested Questions Discuss the questions in the Getting Ready.

- *What does the 0.15 represent?* (the per-minute rental charge of $0.15)

- *What does the 2.50 represent?* (a fixed fee of $2.50 that is charged, regardless of how much time the canoe is used)

Set the scene of students applying for jobs at the boat house and the manager checking to see if they can be trusted to calculate correct rental charges. Read the manager's three questions in the Getting Ready.

- *What is the charge for renting a canoe for 30 minutes?* ($7)

- *A customer is charged $8.50. How long did he use the canoe?* (40 minutes)

- *A customer has $10 to spend. How long can she use a canoe?* (up to 50 minutes)

Suppose you were applying for a job at Sandy's. What strategies would you use to answer these questions? (Collect ideas from students for each question.)

You might list students' suggested strategies on the board or a sheet of chart paper. Students solved problems similar to these in *Moving Straight Ahead*. This is a good time to assess student knowledge of solving linear equations. Many will suggest using a table or a graph. Some may suggest writing and solving an equation. Solving an equation is often the most efficient method for answering questions like these.

Have students work in pairs on Questions A–D of the problem and then have a summary discussion. Question E can be assigned after the summary, as a check of student understanding.

Explore 2.3

As students work, make sure they have viable strategies for both estimating solutions and finding exact solutions. Ask questions to lead them in the right direction as necessary.

Plan your summary as you observe what students can do. The important goal for students is solving equations. If your students seem to understand equation-solving methods and are using them correctly and efficiently, you can focus on inequalities in the summary. If students are struggling with solving equations, do not worry about spending time on inequalities.

Summarize 2.3

As noted in the Explore, you will need to plan your summary depending on the sense students are making of solving equations. The most important thing is for students to have both approximate and exact methods for solving linear equations. Have students share their strategies and discuss them.

Be sure to review how to find solutions to equations using tables, graphs, and symbolic methods.

- *If you have an equation and you know the value of one variable, either x or y, how can you use a graph to estimate the value of the other variable?*

- *How can you use a table to find the value of the other variable?*

- *How can you use an equation to find the value of the other variable?*

Use Question C to revisit the fact-family work from grades 6 and 7. The linear equation $0.15t + 2.5 = 8.50$ can be solved by using a fact-family strategy. Because the fact family for $a + b = c$ includes $a = c - b$, we can write $0.15t = 8.50 - 2.50$, or $0.15t = 6$. Because the fact family for $ab = c$ includes $b = \frac{c}{a}$, we can write $t = \frac{6}{0.15}$, or $t = 40$.

Although it is fairly easy to solve equations of the form $ax + b = c$ by using fact families, it is usually easier to use the rules of equality for equations of the form $ax + b = cx + d$.

Use Question E to practice these ideas.

Few students will have a symbolic method for solving part (2) of Question E. Do not spend too much time on this now. The unit *The Shapes of Algebra* will focus on formal methods for solving inequalities.

If your students are comfortable with equation solving, spend some time on inequalities. Give students inequalities related to the canoe situation, and have them explain what question the inequality represents. For example, the inequality $10 \leq 0.15t + 2.50$ could represent "How long can you rent a canoe for $10 or more?" Ask students how to find solutions to inequalities. Give students a few simple inequalities to solve, for example, $6 \geq 2x$, $10 < x + 1$, and $20 > 2x - 8$. Students can use tables, graphs, or equations to find the solutions. One solution method involves first solving the corresponding equation (for example, $6 = 2x$). Students can then check the values less than, equal to, and greater than the equation's solution to determine which values satisfy the inequality.

2.3 Solving Linear Equations

Mathematical Goals

- Develop skill in solving linear equations with approximation and exact reasoning methods
- Write inequalities to represent "at most" situations

Launch

Introduce the context of renting canoes. On the board or overhead, write $c = 0.15t + 2.50$ and explain what the variables and numbers represent.

Discuss the Getting Ready questions.

List students' suggested strategies for finding answers to the manager's questions on the board or a sheet of chart paper.

Have students work in pairs on Questions A–D of the problem and then have a summary discussion. Question E can be assigned after the summary, as a check of student understanding.

Materials
- Transparency 2.3

Explore

As students work, make sure they have viable strategies for both estimating solutions and finding exact solutions.

Plan your summary based on your observations. If students understand equation-solving methods and are using them correctly and efficiently, focus on inequalities in the summary. If students are struggling with solving equations, do not worry about spending time on inequalities.

Summarize

Review how to find solutions to equations using tables, graphs, or symbolic methods.

- *If you have an equation and you know the value of one variable, either x or y, how can you use a graph to estimate the value of the other variable?*
- *How can you use a table to find the value of the other variable?*
- *How can you use an equation to find the value of the other variable?*

Use Question E to practice these ideas.

If your students are comfortable with equation solving, spend time on inequalities. Give students inequalities related to the canoe situation, and have them explain what question the inequality represents. Give students a few simple inequalities to solve. Students can use tables, graphs, or equations to find the solutions.

Materials
- Student notebooks

Vocabulary
- inequality

Core 20–24
Other *Connections* 43; unassigned choices from previous problems

Adapted For suggestions about adapting ACE exercises, see the CMP *Special Needs Handbook*.

Answers to Problem 2.3

A. For the first question, find the point on the graph with x-coordinate 30. The point is $(30, 7)$. This means that renting a canoe for 30 min costs $7. For the second question, find the point with y-coordinate 8.5. The point is $(40, 8.5)$. This means that for $8.50, you could rent a canoe for 40 min. For the third question, first find the point with a y-coordinate of 10. The point is $(50, 10)$. This means that for exactly $10, you can rent a canoe for 50 min. The customer can rent the canoe for any time of 50 min or less.

B. She could make a table of (*time, charge*) values for 5-min intervals. To answer the three questions, she would need to find the charge value corresponding to the time value 30 and the time values corresponding to the charge value $8.50 and $10. She could make the table with a graphing calculator by entering $y = 0.15x + 2.50$ and setting the x-interval to 1.

C. Yes; she is applying the same operation to both sides of the equation at each step, so the sides remain equal. In the first step, she subtracts 2.50 from each side, or uses the related equation $0.15t = 8.50 - 2.50$. In the second step, she divides both sides by 0.15, or uses the related equation $t = 6.00 \div 0.15$, to get the solution. In the third step, she checks her solution by substituting it into the original equation and making sure the sides of the equation are equal.

D. 1. The charge will be $10 or less for any time from 0 minutes to 50 minutes. This can be seen on a graph of $y = 0.15x + 2.50$ by looking for points on this line that are also on or below the line $y = 10$. It can be seen in a table for $y = 0.15x + 2.50$ by looking for entries with cost values (y-values) less than or equal to 10. To use the equation, solve $10 = 0.15t + 2.50$, which gives $t = 50$; then test t-values less than 50 in the inequality to see that the solution is $t \leq 50$.

2. The solution is all the t-values less than or equal to 50. This can be represented as $t \leq 50$. (Note that the model $1.5t + 2.50 \leq 50$ does not match the context for all values of t because time is nonnegative.)

E. 1. 50 min; the solution of $9 = 4 + 0.10t$ is $t = 50$.

2. At most, 80 min; the solution of $4 + 0.10t \leq 12$ is $t \leq 80$.

3. $6; $4 + 0.10(20) = 6$

2.4 Intersecting Linear Models

Goal

- Use equations to represent questions about problem situations and interpret the solutions in the context of the problem

This problem gives students a chance to put together what they learned and reviewed in the previous three problems.

Launch 2.4

Introduce the context of the resort area with an amusement park and movie theater.

Suggested Questions Ask students for their ideas about what variables affect attendance. Then focus specifically on the rain forecast.

- *How might the probability of rain affect attendance at the amusement park?* (Attendance is likely to be higher when the chance of rain is low.)

- *How might the probability of rain affect attendance at the movie theater?* (Attendance is likely to be higher when the chance of rain is high.)

Then have students look at the table of (*rain probability, attendance*) data.

- *Do your ideas match the trend in the data?*

Explain to students that Problem 2.4 asks them to analyze the patterns in the data and to make predictions.

Have students work in pairs or groups of three.

Explore 2.4

Suggested Questions If students are not sure how to begin, ask questions to remind them how to find the linear equations called for at the start of the problem.

- *What would a plot of these data look like?*

- *What do you need to know to find the equation of a line?*

If students write the probability in decimal form, point out that the probabilities in the table are given as percents. The equation will produce a probability as a percent, and there is no need to use decimals.

You might have students make their plots and lines on transparent grids. Students can use the graphs during the summary to help explain how they found the equations.

Summarize 2.4

Have students display their graphs and share the strategies they used to find the equations.

In answering Question B, students may use numerical or graphical approximation methods (perhaps by using a graphing calculator to generate and trace tables and graphs), or they may use symbolic reasoning alone. Be sure both methods are discussed.

Suggested Question

- *What strategies can you use to find solutions to linear equations?* (Trace a graph or table to get estimates of the answers or use symbolic reasoning to find exact answers.)

If only one method is offered, ask students for ideas about how the other approaches would be useful, and carry them out to see whether the results agree. In general, numerical or graphical approaches will yield only approximations.

The discussion of Question B will allow you to assess how confident your students are at solving linear equations.

For part (4) of Question B, do not expect students to solve the system of equations symbolically; they likely will not. (Solving systems of equations will be taught formally in *The Shapes of Algebra*.) However, it is a good idea to present the possibility of doing so. Students may be able to understand how to represent the situation symbolically, even if they cannot yet solve it that way.

Because students are looking for the point at which attendance at the two attractions is the same, they could set the equations equal to one another and solve the resulting linear equation.

Big Fun = Get Reel

$$A_B = A_G$$

$$1,000 - 7.5r = 300 + 2r$$

Then ask:

- *What question does this equation represent?* (For what probability of rain will the predicted attendance be the same at both the amusement park and the theater?)

- *How could you estimate the solution using a table?* (For a calculator table, enter $y = 1,000 - 7.5x$ and $y = 300 + 2x$ and find a row for which the values of Y1 and Y2 are the same. The X value for this row is the solution. For a hand-drawn table, find y-values for x-values in regular intervals. You might have to check between table values to get an accurate solution.)

- *How could you estimate the solution using a graph?* (For a calculator graph, enter $y = 1,000 - 7.5x$ and $y = 300 + 2x$ and display the graphs in the same window. Trace to find the point where the lines intersect. The x-coordinate of the intersection point is the answer. For a hand-drawn graph, graph both equations on the same axes and estimate the x-coordinate of the intersection point.)

- *How could you find the solution symbolically?* (If $1,000 - 7.5r = 300 + 2r$, then $700 = 9.5r$; $74 \approx r$.)

2.4 Intersecting Linear Models

Mathematical Goal

- Use equations to represent questions about problem situations and interpret the solutions in the context of the problem

Launch

Introduce the context of the amusement park and movie theater.

- *How might the probability of rain affect attendance at the amusement park?*
- *How might the probability of rain affect attendance at the movie theater?*

Have students look at the table of (*rain probability, attendance*) data.

- *Do your ideas match the trend of the data?*

Explain to students that Problem 2.4 asks them to analyze the patterns in the data and make predictions.

Have students work in pairs or groups of three.

Explore

- *What would a plot of these data look like?*
- *What do you need to know to find the equation of a line?*

If students write the probability in decimal form, point out that the probabilities in the table are given as percents. The equation will produce a probability as a percent, and there is no need to use decimals.

You might have students make their plots and lines on transparent grids or chart paper. Students can use the graphs during the summary to help explain how they fit the lines and found the equations.

Materials
- Transparent grids or chart paper (optional)
- Graphing calculator (optional)

Summarize

Have students display their graphs and share the strategies.

For Question B, students may use numerical or graphical approximation methods (perhaps by using a graphing calculator to generate and trace tables and graphs), or they may use symbolic reasoning. Be sure both methods are discussed.

If only one method is offered, ask students how the other approaches would be useful and carry them out to see whether the results agree.

The discussion of Question B will allow you to assess how confident your students are at solving linear equations.

Materials
- Student notebooks

continued on next page

Summarize
continued

For part (4) of Question B, do not expect students to solve the system of equations symbolically. However, it is a good idea to present the possibility of doing so. Students may be able to understand how to represent the situation symbolically, even if they cannot yet solve that way. You could write:

Big Fun = Get Reel

$$A_B = A_G$$

$$1{,}000 - 7.5r = 300 + 2r$$

- *What question does this equation represent?*
- *How could you estimate the solution using a table? Using a graph?*
- *How could you find the solution symbolically?*

ACE Assignment Guide for Problem 2.4

Differentiated Instruction
Solutions for All Learners

Core 25–28, 33, 34, 44–52
Other *Applications* 29–32; *Connections* 53–56; unassigned choices from previous problems

Adapted For suggestions about adapting ACE exercises, see the CMP *Special Needs Handbook*.
Connecting to Prior Units 44–52: *Accentuate the Negative*; 54: *Variables and Patterns*; 55: *Stretching and Shrinking*

Answers to Problem 2.4

A. 1. $A_B \approx 1{,}000 - 7.5p$

  2. $A_G \approx 300 + 2p$

B. 1. $A_B = 625$ people and $A_G = 400$ people

  2. 72%

  3. Solve $300 + 2p \geq 360$, which gives $p \geq 30$. So, a probability of rain of at least 30% will lead to movie attendance of at least 360.

  4. Solve $1{,}000 - 7.5p = 300 + 2p$, or graph both equations and find the intersection point. This occurs when $p \approx 74$, so, for a probability of rain of about 74%, the predicted attendance is the same at both attractions.

The student edition pages for this
investigation begin on the next page.

Notes _____

_____

_____

_____

Linear Models and Equations

Organizing and displaying the data from an experiment or survey can help you spot trends and make predictions. When the data show a linear trend, you can find a graph and equation to *model* the relationship between the variables. You can then use the model to make predictions about values between and beyond the data values.

When you make a model to represent a mathematical relationship, examine your model and ask

For what interval of values is the model likely to be reasonably accurate?

2.1 Linear Models

The First State Bridge-Painting Company is often asked to bid on painting projects. It usually gets the contract if it offers the lowest price. However, it needs to make sure the bid is high enough that the company will make a reasonable profit.

First State is preparing a bid for a bridge-painting project. The company looks at its records for previous projects. It finds information about four bridges with similar designs.

First State Bridge-Painting Costs		
Bridge Number	**Length (ft)**	**Painting Cost**
1	100	$18,000
2	200	$37,000
3	300	$48,000
4	400	$66,000

24   Thinking With Mathematical Models

STUDENT PAGE

Notes _____

_____

_____

_____

(24) 54

The First State cost estimators plot the data. The points fall in a nearly linear pattern. They draw a line that fits the pattern well. The line is a **mathematical model** for the relationship between bridge length and painting cost. A mathematical model approximates a data pattern.

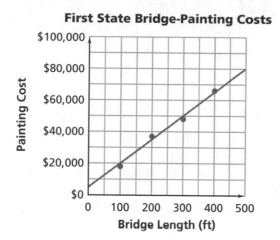

First State Bridge-Painting Costs

Getting Ready for Problem 2.1

A mathematical model can be used to make predictions about values between and beyond the data points.

- How do you think the cost estimators decided where to draw the line?
- Is the line a reasonable model for these data?
- What information does the model give that the points alone do not?
- What questions could you answer using the model?
- What information do you need to write an equation for the line?

Problem 2.1 Linear Models

A. 1. Write an equation for the line that models the data.

 2. Use the line or the equation to estimate painting costs for similar bridges that are

 a. 175 feet long **b.** 280 feet long

 3. Use the line or the equation to estimate lengths of similar bridges for which the painting costs are

 a. $10,000 **b.** $60,000

Investigation 2 Linear Models and Equations **25**

Notes

B. First State is also bidding on a different type of bridge. It has records for three similar bridges.

First State Bridge-Painting Costs

Bridge Number	Length (ft)	Painting Cost
3	150	$50,000
4	300	$80,000
5	500	$140,000

1. Plot these data points. Draw a line that models the pattern in the data points.

2. Write an equation for your line.

3. Use your equation or line to estimate the painting cost for a similar bridge that is 200 feet long.

4. Use your equation or line to estimate the length of a similar bridge that costs $100,000 to paint.

ACE **Homework starts on page 33.**

Notes _____

_____

_____

_____

Equations for Linear Relationships

Cars and trucks are an important part of American life and culture. There are nearly 200 million licensed drivers and 140 million registered passenger cars in the United States. To help people keep their cars clean, many cities have self-service car washes.

At most self-service car washes, the charge for washing a car and the company's profit depend on the time the customer spends using the car wash. To run such a business efficiently, it helps to have equations relating these key variables.

Getting Ready for Problem 2.2

- Sudzo Wash and Wax charges customers $0.75 per minute to wash a car. Write an equation that relates the total charge c to the amount of time t in minutes.

- Pat's Power Wash charges $2.00 per car to cover the cost of cleaning supplies, plus $0.49 per minute for the use of water sprayers and vacuums. Write an equation for the total charge c for any car-wash time t.

- U-Wash-It charges $10 for each car. The business owners estimate that it costs them $0.60 per minute to provide soap, water, and vacuums for a car. Write an equation for the profit p U-Wash-It earns if a customer spends t minutes washing a car.

- Explain what the numbers and variables in each equation represent.

- What questions can your equations help you answer?

Notes _____

_____

_____

A. The Squeaky Clean Car Wash charges by the minute. This table shows the charges for several different times.

Squeaky Clean Car Wash Charges

Time (min)	5	10	15	20	25
Charge	$8	$13	$18	$23	$28

1. Explain how you know the relationship is linear.

2. What are the slope and *y*-intercept of the line that represents the data?

3. Write an equation relating charge *c* to time *t* in minutes.

B. Euclid's Car Wash displays its charges as a graph. Write an equation for the charge plan at Euclid's. Describe what the variables and numbers in your equation tell you about the situation.

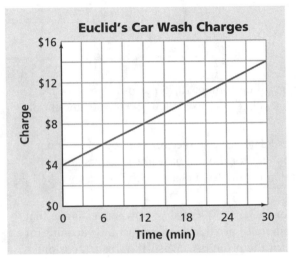

Euclid's Car Wash Charges

28   Thinking With Mathematical Models

Notes _____

_____

_____

_____

C. Below are two receipts from Super Clean Car Wash. Assume the relationship between charge c and time used t is linear.

```
vvvvvvvvvvvvvvvvvvvvv
      SUPER CLEAN
       Car Wash
    Date:  3-14-05
    Start time:  01:55 pm
    Stop time:  02:05 pm
    Charge:  $7.00
AAAAAAAAAAAAAAAAAAAAA
```

```
vvvvvvvvvvvvvvvvvvvvv
      SUPER CLEAN
       Car Wash
    Date:  4-04-05
    Start time:  09:30 am
    Stop time:  09:50 am
    Charge:  $12.00
AAAAAAAAAAAAAAAAAAAAA
```

1. Each receipt represents a point (t, c) on the line. Find the coordinates of the two points.

2. What are the slope and y-intercept of the line?

3. Write an equation relating c and t.

D. Write an equation for the line with slope -3 that passes through the point $(4, 3)$.

E. Write an equation for the line with points $(4, 5)$ and $(6, 9)$.

F. Suppose you want to write an equation of the form $y = mx + b$ to represent a linear relationship. What is your strategy if you are given

1. a description of the relationship in words?

2. two or more (x, y) values or a table of (x, y) values?

3. a graph showing points with coordinates?

ACE **Homework starts on page 33.**

Notes _____

_____

_____

_____

Sandy's Boat House rents canoes. The equation $c = 0.15t + 2.50$ gives the charge c in dollars for renting a canoe for t minutes.

Getting Ready for Problem 2.3

- Explain what the numbers in the equation $c = 0.15t + 2.50$ tell you about the situation.

- Rashida and Serena apply for jobs at Sandy's. The manager tests them with three questions.

  What is the charge for renting a canoe for 30 minutes?

  A customer is charged $8.50. How long did he use the canoe?

  A customer has $10 to spend. How long can she use a canoe?

  Suppose you were applying for a job at Sandy's. How would you answer these questions?

Problem 2.3 Solving Linear Equations

A. Rashida uses a graph of $c = 0.15t + 2.50$. Explain how to use the graph to estimate the answers to the manager's questions.

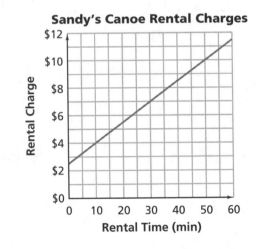

Sandy's Canoe Rental Charges

Notes _____

_____

_____

_____

B. Rashida could use a table instead of a graph. Explain how to use a table to estimate answers to the questions.

C. Serena wants to find exact answers, not estimates. For the second question, she solves the linear equation $0.15t + 2.50 = 8.50$. She reasons as follows:

- If $0.15t + 2.50 = 8.50$, then $0.15t = 6.00$.
- If $0.15t = 6.00$, then $t = 40$.
- I check my answer by substituting 40 for t: $0.15(40) + 2.50 = 8.50$

Is Serena correct? How do you know?

D. For the third question, Rashida says, "She can use the canoe for 50 minutes if she has $10." Serena says there are other possibilities— for example, 45 minutes or 30 minutes. She says you can answer the question by solving the **inequality** $0.15t + 2.50 \leq 10$. This inequality represents the times for which the rental charge is *at most* $10.

1. Use a table, a graph, and the equation $0.15t + 2.50 = 10$ to find all of the times for which the inequality is true.

2. Express the solution as an inequality.

E. River Fun Paddle Boats competes with Sandy's. The equation $c = 4 + 0.10t$ gives the charge in dollars c for renting a paddle boat for t minutes.

1. A customer at River Fun is charged $9. How long did the customer use a paddle boat? Explain.

2. Suppose you want to spend $12 at most. How long could you use a paddle boat? Explain.

3. What is the charge to rent a paddle boat for 20 minutes? Explain.

ACE Homework starts on page 33.

Notes _____

_____

_____

_____

2.4 Intersecting Linear Models

A resort area has two main attractions—the Big Fun amusement park and the Get Reel movie multiplex. The number of visitors to each attraction on a given day is related to the probability of rain.

This table gives attendance and rain-forecast data for several Saturdays.

Saturday Resort Attendance

Probability of Rain (%)	0	20	40	60	80	100
Big Fun Attendance	1,000	850	700	550	400	250
Get Reel Attendance	300	340	380	420	460	500

The same company owns both businesses. The managers want to be able to predict Saturday attendance at each attraction so they can assign their workers efficiently.

Problem 2.4 Intersecting Linear Models

A. Use the table to find a linear equation relating the probability of rain p to

  1. Saturday attendance A_B at Big Fun.

  2. Saturday attendance A_G at Get Reel.

B. Use your equations from Question A to answer these questions. Show your calculations and explain your reasoning.

  1. Suppose there is a 50% probability of rain this Saturday. What is the expected attendance at each attraction?

  2. Suppose 460 people visited Big Fun one Saturday. Estimate the probability of rain on that day.

  3. What probability of rain would give a predicted Saturday attendance of at least 360 people at Get Reel?

  4. Is there a probability of rain for which the predicted attendance is the same at both attractions? Explain.

ACE Homework starts on page 33.

Notes _____

_____

_____

_____

Applications

1. Below are some results from the bridge-thickness experiment.

Bridge-Thickness Experiment

Thickness (layers)	2	4	6	8
Breaking Weight (pennies)	15	30	50	65

a. Plot the (*thickness, breaking weight*) data. Draw a line that models the pattern in the data.

b. Find an equation for the line you drew.

c. Use your equation to predict the breaking weights of paper bridges 3, 5, and 7 layers thick.

2. Which line do you think is a better model for the data? Explain.

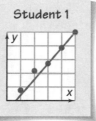

3. Copy each graph onto grid paper. Draw a line that fits each set of data as closely as possible. Describe the strategies you used.

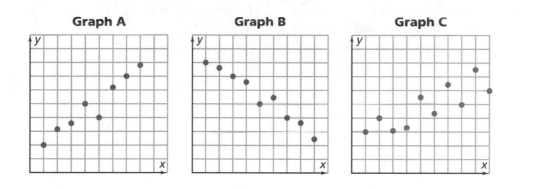

Notes _____

_____

_____

_____

4. This table gives the average weights of purebred Chihuahuas from birth to 16 weeks.

Average Weights for Chihuahuas

Age (wk)	0	2	4	6	8	10	12	14	16
Weight (oz)	4	9	13	17.5	21.5	25	30	34	39

SOURCE: *The Complete Chihuahua Encyclopedia*

a. Graph the (*age, weight*) data. Draw a line that models the data pattern.

b. Write an equation of the form $y = mx + b$ for your line. Explain what the values of m and b tell you about this situation.

c. Use your equation to predict the average weight of Chihuahuas for odd-numbered ages from 1 to 15 weeks.

d. What average weight does your linear model predict for a Chihuahua that is 144 weeks old? Explain why this prediction is unlikely to be accurate.

5. U-Wash-It Car Wash did market research to determine how much to charge for a car wash. The company makes this table based on its findings.

Homework
Help Online
PHSchool.com
For: Help with Exercise 5
Web Code: ape-1205

U-Wash-It Projections

Price per Wash	$0	$5	$10	$15	$20
Customers Expected per Day	100	80	65	45	20

a. Graph the (*price, expected customers*) data. Draw a line that models the data pattern.

b. Write an equation in the form $y = mx + b$ for your graph. Explain what the values of m and b tell you about this situation.

c. Use your equation to estimate the number of customers expected for prices of $2.50, $7.50, and $12.50.

Notes _____

_____

_____

_____

6. Find the slope, y-intercept, and equation for each line.

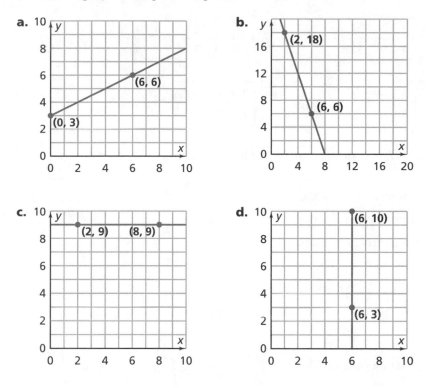

The relationships in Exercises 7–10 are linear.

7. a. A typical American baby weighs about 8 pounds at birth and gains about 1.5 pounds per month for the first year of life. What equation relates weight w in pounds to age a in months?

   b. Can this model be used to predict weight at age 80? Explain.

8. Kaya buys a $20 phone card. She is charged $0.15 per minute for long-distance calls. What equation gives the value v left on her card after she makes t minutes of long-distance calls?

9. Dakota lives 1,500 meters from school. She leaves for school, walking at a speed of 60 meters per minute. Write an equation for her distance d in meters from school after she walks for t minutes.

10. A car can average 140 miles on 5 gallons of gasoline. Write an equation for the distance d in miles the car can travel on g gallons of gas.

Investigation 2 Linear Models and Equations   **35**

Notes

11. Write a linear equation for each table relating x and y.

a.
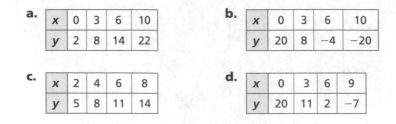

x	0	3	6	10
y	2	8	14	22

b.

x	0	3	6	10
y	20	8	−4	−20

c.

x	2	4	6	8
y	5	8	11	14

d.

x	0	3	6	9
y	20	11	2	−7

For Exercises 12–17, find an equation for the line that satisfies the conditions.

12. Slope 4.2; y-intercept $(0, 3.4)$

13. Slope $\frac{2}{3}$; y-intercept $(0, 5)$

14. Slope 2; passes through $(4, 12)$

15. Passes through $(0, 15)$ and $(5, 3)$

16. Passes through $(-2, 2)$ and $(5, -4)$

17. Parallel to the line with equation $y = 15 - 2x$ and passes through $(3, 0)$

18. Write an equation for each line.

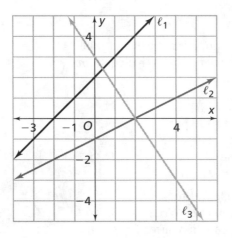

Notes _____

_____

_____

_____

19. Anchee and Jonah earn weekly allowances for doing chores over the summer.

- Anchee's father pays her $5 each week.
- Jonah's mother paid him $20 at the beginning of the summer and now pays him $3 each week.

The relationships between number of weeks worked and dollars earned are shown in this graph.

Earnings From Chores

a. Which line represents Jonah's earnings? Which line represents Anchee's earnings? Explain.

b. Write two linear equations in the form $y = mx + b$ to show the relationships between Anchee's earnings and the number of weeks she works and between Jonah's earnings and the number of weeks he works.

c. What do the values of m and b in each equation tell about the relationship between the number of weeks and the dollars earned?

d. What do the values of m and b tell about each line?

Investigation 2 Linear Models and Equations **37**

STUDENT PAGE

Notes _____

_____

_____

_____

(37) 54

For Exercises 20–23, do the following:

    a. Solve the equation. Show your steps.

    b. Graph the associated line (for example, for $5.5x + 32 = 57$, graph $y = 5.5x + 32$). Label the point that shows the solution.

20. $5.5x + 32 = 57$ **21.** $-24 = 4x - 12$

22. $5x - 51 = 24$ **23.** $74 = 53 - 7x$

24. At Water Works Amusement Park, the daily profit from the concession stands depends on the number of park visitors. The equation $p = 2.50v - 500$ gives the estimated profit p in dollars if v people visit the park. In parts (a)–(c), use a graph to estimate the answer. Then, find the answer by writing and solving an equation or inequality.

    a. For what number of visitors will the profit be about $2,000?

    b. One day 200 people visit the park. What is the approximate concession-stand profit for that day?

    c. For what number of visitors will the profit be at least $500?

25. The following formulas give the fare f in dollars that two bus companies charge for trips of d miles.

    Transcontinental: $f = 0.15d + 12$

    Intercity Express: $f = 5 + 0.20d$

    In parts (a)–(c), use a graph to estimate the answer. Then, find the answer by writing and solving an equation or inequality.

    a. For Transcontinental, how many miles is a trip that costs $99?

    b. For Intercity Express, how far can a person travel for a fare that is at most $99?

    c. Is there a distance for which the fare for the two bus lines is the same? If so, give the distance and the fare.

Solve each equation. Show the steps in your solutions.

26. $5x + 7 = 3x - 5$ **27.** $7 + 3x = 5x - 5$ **28.** $2.5x - 8 = 5x + 12$

Find at least three values of x for which the inequality is true.

29. $4x \leq 12$ **30.** $3x < 18$

31. $4x + 5 \leq 13$ **32.** $3x - 9 \leq 18$

Notes _____

_____

_____

_____

33. Every Friday, the mechanic for Columbus Public Schools records the miles driven and the gallons of gas used for each school bus. One week, the mechanic records these data.

Data for Columbus Bus Fleet

Bus Number	1	2	3	4	5	6	7	8
Gas Used (gal)	5	8	12	15	18	20	22	25
Miles Driven	80	100	180	225	280	290	320	375

a. Write a linear equation that models the relationship between miles driven d and gallons of gas used g.

b. Use your equation to predict the number of miles such a bus could travel on 10 gallons of gas.

c. Use your equation to predict the number of gallons of gas required to drive such a bus 250 miles.

d. What do the values of m and b in your equation $d = mg + b$ tell about the fuel efficiency of the school bus fleet?

34. One of the most popular items at a farmers' market is sweet corn. This table shows relationships among the price for the corn, the demand for the corn (how much corn people want to buy), and the leftovers of corn (how much corn the market has at the end of the day).

Sweet Corn Supply and Demand

Price per Dozen	$1	$1.50	$2.00	$2.50	$3.00	$3.50
Demand (dozens)	200	175	140	120	80	60
Leftovers (dozens)	40	75	125	175	210	260

a. Why do you think the demand for corn decreases as the price goes up?

b. Why do you think the leftovers of corn increases as the price goes up?

c. Write a linear equation that models the relationship between demand d and price p.

d. Write a linear equation that models the relationship between leftovers ℓ and price p.

e. Use graphs to estimate the price for which the leftovers equals the demand. Then, find the price by solving symbolically.

Investigation 2 Linear Models and Equations   **39**

STUDENT PAGE

Notes _____

(39) 54

Connections

35. Tell whether each table represents a linear relationship. Explain.

a.

x	2	4	6	8	10	12	14
y	0	1	2	3	4	5	6

b.

x	1	2	3	4	5	6	7
y	0	3	8	15	24	35	48

c.

x	1	4	6	7	10	12	16
y	2	−1	−3	−4	−7	−9	−13

36. For parts (a)–(d), copy the table. Then, use the equation to complete the table. Tell whether the relationship is linear. Explain.

a. $y = -3x - 8$

b. $y = 4(x - 7) + 6$

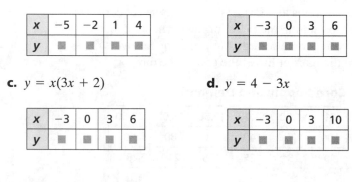

x	−5	−2	1	4
y	▪	▪	▪	▪

x	−3	0	3	6
y	▪	▪	▪	▪

c. $y = x(3x + 2)$

d. $y = 4 - 3x$

x	−3	0	3	6
y	▪	▪	▪	▪

x	−3	0	3	10
y	▪	▪	▪	▪

Copy each pair of numbers in Exercises 37–42. Insert <, >, or = to make a true statement.

37. −5 ▪ 3

38. $\frac{2}{3}$ ▪ $\frac{1}{2}$

39. $\frac{9}{12}$ ▪ $\frac{3}{4}$

40. 3.009 ▪ 3.1

41. $\frac{-2}{3}$ ▪ $\frac{-1}{2}$

42. −4.25 ▪ −2.45

STUDENT PAGE

Notes _____

_____

_____

_____

43. Madeline sets a copy machine to enlarge by a factor of 150%. She then uses the machine to copy a polygon. Write an equation that relates the perimeter of the polygon after the enlargement a to the perimeter before the enlargement b.

For Exercises 44–52, evaluate the expression without using a calculator.

44. $-15 + (-7)$ **45.** $-7 - 15$ **46.** $-7 - (-15)$

47. $-15 + 7$ **48.** $-20 \div 5$ **49.** $-20 \div (-5)$

50. $20 \div (-4)$ **51.** $-20 \div (-2.5)$ **52.** $-20 \cdot (-2.5)$

53. You can express the slope of a line in different ways. The slope of the line below is $\frac{6}{10}$, or 0.6. You can also say the slope is 60% because the rise is 60% of the run.

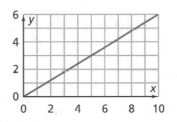

These numbers represent slopes of lines.

$\frac{-4}{-2}$ 60% $\frac{4}{4}$ 1.5   150%   200%

a. Which numbers represent the same slope?

b. Which number represents the greatest slope? Which represents the least slope?

Investigation 2 Linear Models and Equations   **41**

Notes _____

_____

_____

_____

54. Consider the following stories and the graphs.

a. Match each story with a graph. Tell how you would label the axes. Explain how each part of the story is represented in the graph.

Story 1 A parachutist is taken up in a plane. After he jumps, the wind blows him off course. He ends up tangled in the branches of a tree.

Story 2 Ella puts some money in the bank. She leaves it there to earn interest for several years. Then one day, she withdraws half of the money in the account.

Story 3 Gerry has a big pile of gravel to spread on his driveway. On the first day, he moves half of the gravel from the pile to his driveway. The next day he is tired and moves only half of what is left. The third day he again moves half of what is left in the pile. He continues in this way until the pile has almost disappeared.

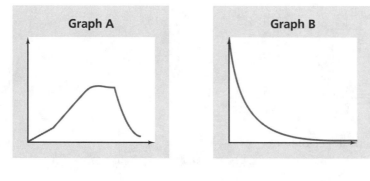

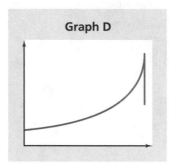

b. One of the graphs does not match a story. Make up your own story for that graph.

Notes _____

_____

_____

_____

55. The figures below are similar.

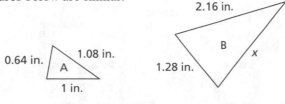

a. Find x.

b. What is the scale factor from Triangle A to Triangle B?

c. What is the scale factor from Triangle B to Triangle A?

d. How are the scale factors in parts (b) and (c) related?

Extensions

56. A bridge-painting company uses the formula $C = 5,000 + 150L$ to estimate painting costs. C is the cost in dollars, and L is the length of the bridge in feet. To make a profit, the company increases a cost estimate by 20% to arrive at a bid price. For example, if the cost estimate is $10,000, the bid price will be $12,000.

a. Find bid prices for bridges 100 feet, 200 feet, and 400 feet long.

b. Write a formula relating the final bid price to bridge length.

c. Use your formula to find bid prices for bridges 150 feet, 300 feet, and 450 feet long.

d. How would your formula change if the markup for profit was 15% instead of 20%?

57. Recall that Custom Steel Products builds beams from steel rods. Here is a 7-foot beam.

7-foot beam made from 27 rods

a. Which of these formulas represents the relationship between beam length ℓ and number of rods r?

$r = 3\ell$ $r = \ell + (\ell - 1) + 2\ell$

$r = 4(\ell - 1) + 3$ $r = 4\ell - 1$

b. How might you have reasoned to come up with each formula?

Notes _____

_____

_____

_____

58. Recall that Custom Steel Products uses steel rods to make staircase frames. Here are staircase frames with 1, 2, and 3 steps.

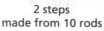
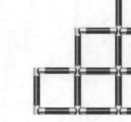
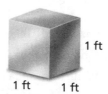

| 1 step | 2 steps | 3 steps |
| made from 4 rods | made from 10 rods | made from 18 rods |

Which of these formulas represents the relationship between the number of steps n and number of rods r?

$r = n^2 + 3n$ $r = n(n + 3)$

$r = n^2 + 3$ $r = (n + 3)n$

Custom Steel Products builds cubes out of square steel plates measuring 1 foot on a side. At right is a 1-foot cube. Use this information for Exercises 59–61.

59. How many square plates are needed to make a 1-foot cube?

60. Multiple Choice Suppose CSP wants to triple the dimensions of the cube. How many times the number of plates in the original cube will they need for this larger cube?

A. 2   **B.** 3   **C.** 4   **D.** 9

61. Multiple Choice Suppose CSP triples the dimensions of the original cube. How many times the volume of the original cube is the volume of the new cube?

F. 8   **G.** 9   **H.** 27   **J.** 81

62. At Yvonne's Auto Detailing, car washes cost $5 for any time up to 10 minutes, plus $0.40 per minute after that. The managers at Yvonne's are trying to agree on a formula for calculating the cost c for a t-minute car wash.

a. Sid thinks $c = 0.4t + 5$ is correct. Is he right?

b. Tina proposes the formula $c = 0.4(t - 10) + 5$. Is she right?

c. Jamal told Tina her formula could be simplified to $c = 0.4t + 1$. Is he right?

44   Thinking With Mathematical Models

Notes _____

_____

_____

_____

63. Write an equation for each relationship.

a. The Bluebird Taxi Company charges $1.50 for the first 2 miles of any trip, and then $1.20 for each mile after that. How is the taxi *fare* related to the *distance* of a trip?

b. An airport offers free parking for 30 minutes and then charges $2.00 for each hour after that. How is the *price* for parking related to the *time* a car is parked?

c. The Regal Cinema makes $6.50 on each ticket sold. However, it has operating expenses of $750 per day. How is *daily profit* related to *number of tickets* sold?

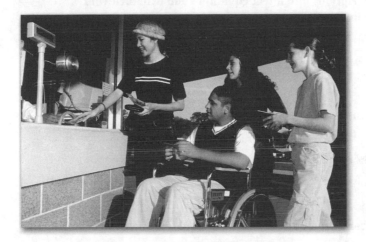

d. Rush Computer Repair sends technicians to businesses to fix computers. They charge a fixed fee of $50, plus $50 per hour. How is total *cost* for a repair related to *time* the repair takes?

Notes _____

_____

_____

_____

Mathematical Reflections 2

In this investigation, you learned how to find linear models for data patterns. You also developed skill in writing linear equations, practiced translating verbal descriptions into linear equations, and extended your knowledge of solving linear equations.

Think about your answers to these questions. Discuss your ideas with other students and your teacher. Then write a summary of your findings in your notebook.

1. What are the advantages of using a linear model for a set of data?

2. How would you find the equation for a linear relationship
   a. from a verbal description?
   b. from a table of values?
   c. from a graph?

3. What strategies can you use to solve a linear equation such as
   a. $500 = 245 + 5x$?
   b. $500 + 3x = 245 + 5x$?

Notes

Answers Applications Connections Extensions

Investigation 2

ACE
Assignment Choices

Differentiated Instruction
Solutions for All Learners

Problem 2.1
Core 1, 2, 3
Other *Connections* 35, 36

Problem 2.2
Core 5–17
Other *Applications* 4, 18, 19; *Connections* 37–42;
Extensions 57–63; unassigned choices from
previous problems

Problem 2.3
Core 20–24
Other *Connections* 43; unassigned choices from
previous problems

Problem 2.4
Core 25–28, 33, 34, 44–52
Other *Applications* 29–32; *Connections* 53–56;
unassigned choices from previous problems

Adapted For suggestions about adapting ACE
exercises, see the CMP *Special Needs Handbook*.
Connecting to Prior Units 35, 36: *Moving Straight
Ahead*; 44–52: *Accentuate the Negative*; 43, 55:
Stretching and Shrinking; 54: *Variables and Patterns*

Applications

1. a. Accept any line that approximates the data.
Here is one possibility:

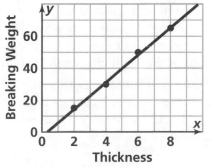

Arkansas Bridge–Thickness Experiment

b. Possible answer: $y = 8.5x - 2.5$. Students
might come up with a simpler model with
a y-intercept of 0, such as $y = 8x$ (because
0 thickness should suggest 0 strength).

c. Answers depend on the equation. Using the
preceding equation, the breaking weights
are 23, 40, and 57.

2. Student 1's line is a better fit. Overall, the
data points are closer to Student 1's line. Also,
the slope of Student 1's line seems to better
match the rate of change in the data points.

3. Lines and strategies will vary. Note that
Labsheet 2ACE Exercise 3 includes
Graphs A–C, plus six additional graphs. When
you look at Graphs A, B, C, D, and F from left
to right, you see a definite linear trend in the
data; these data can be modeled with a straight
line. The points in Graph E might represent a
linear relationship, but they might be better
modeled with a curve, especially toward the
right part of the graph. The relationships in
Graphs G, H, and I are definitely not linear.
The points in G and H show nonlinear trend.
The points in I do not seem to show any
trend; they bounce all around.

4. a. Lines will vary. Here is one possibility:

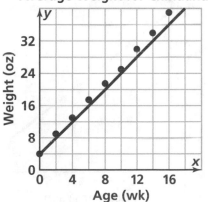

Average Weight for Chihuahuas

b. Possible answer: $y = 2.2x + 4$. The value of m indicates that on average, a Chihuahua grows 2 oz per wk. To find this value, students may notice that as the age changes by 2 wk, the weight usually changes by about 4 oz. The value of b indicates that the weight of a Chihuahua at birth is 4 oz.

c. The model $y = 2.2x + 4$ gives the following estimates:

Age (wk)	Weight (oz)
1	6
3	10.5
5	15
7	19.5
9	23.5
11	28
13	32.5
15	37

d. Answers depend on the model from part (b). The model $y = 2.2x + 4$ predicts a weight of 321 oz or 20 lb for a 36-mo-old Chihuahua. In reality, a Chihuahua of this age is full grown and typically weighs only 4 lb. This error of prediction illustrates the danger of using a data-based model to make predictions far beyond the data on which the model was based.

5. a. Lines will vary. Possible answer:

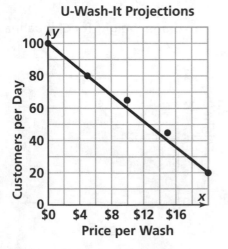

U-Wash-It Projections

b. Possible equation: $y = 100 - 4x$. The 100 means that if the car wash were free, there

would be about 100 customers per day. The -4 means that for each \$1 increase in price, there would be a decrease of about 4 customers per day.

c. \$2.50: 90; \$7.50: 70; \$12.50: 50

6. Note: Many students find parts (c) and (d) challenging. You may want to discuss these.

a. Slope: 0.5, y-intercept: 3; $y = 0.5x + 3$

b. Slope: -3, y-intercept: 24; $y = -3x + 24$

c. Slope: 0, y-intercept: 9; $y = 9$

d. Slope: undefined, y-intercept: none; $x = 6$.

7. a. $w = 8 + 1.5a$

b. No. A person would weigh 1,448 pounds when he reaches 80, according to the model.

8. $v = 20 - 0.15t$

9. $d = 1500 - 60t$ **10.** $d = 28g$

11. a. $y = 2x + 2$ **b.** $y = -4x + 20$

     c. $y = 1.5x + 2$ **d.** $y = -3x + 20$

12. $y = 4.2x + 3.4$ **13.** $y = \frac{2}{3}x + 5$

14. $y = 2x + 4$

15. $y = -\frac{12}{5}x + 15$ or $y = -2.4x + 15$

16. $y = \frac{-6}{7}x + \frac{2}{7}$ **17.** $y = -2x + 6$

18. $\ell_1: y = x + 2; \ell_2: 0.5x - 1; \ell_3: -1.5x + 3$

19. a. The graph that has y-intercept $(0, 0)$ shows Anchee's earnings because her father does not pay her any money at the beginning of the summer. The graph that has y-intercept $(0, 20)$ shows Jonah's earnings because he gets \$20 at the beginning of the summer. On the graph, we can see that Anchee's earnings increase by \$5 per week and Jonah's by \$3 per week.

b. Anchee: $y = 5x$
Jonah: $y = 20 + 3x$

c. The value of m in each case tells the rate at which earnings increase per week. The value of b is the amount of money each student received at the beginning of the summer.

d. The value of b is the y-coordinate of the point where the graph crosses the y-axis. That is, it is the y-intercept. The value of m is the slope of the line.

20. $x \approx 4.54$

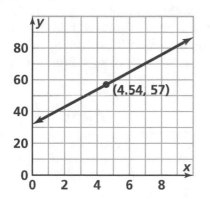

21. $x = -3$

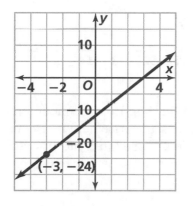

22. $x = 15$

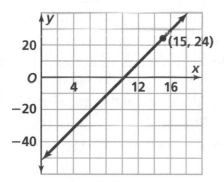

23. $x = -3$

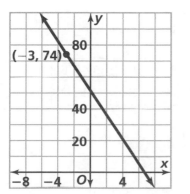

24.

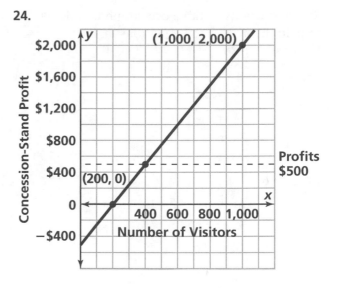

a. About 1,000 visitors; $2,000 = 2.5v - 500$, so $v = 1,000$ visitors

b. About 0; $p = 2.50(200) - 500 = 0$

c. $v \geq 400$; on the graph, the profit is greater than $500 for all points on or above the dashed line; solve $2.50v - 500 \geq 500$.

25.

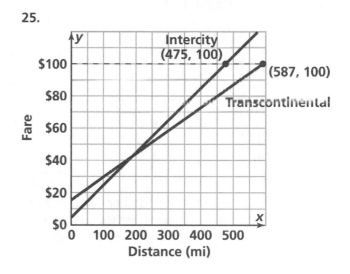

a. 580 mi; $99 = 0.15d + 12$, so $d = 580$ mi

b. 470 mi; $99 = 5 + 0.20d$, so $d = 470$ mi

c. Yes; about 140 mi and $33; $0.15d + 12 = 5 + 0.20d$, so $d = 140$

Students can use a table or a graphing calculator to help them solve the equations in Exercises 26–28.

26. $x = -6$

$$5x + 7 = 3x - 5$$
$$5x = 3x - 12$$
$$2x = -12$$
$$x = -6$$

27. $x = 6$

$$7 + 3x = 5x - 5$$
$$12 + 3x = 5x$$
$$12 = 2x$$
$$6 = x$$

28. $x = -8$

$$2.5x - 8 = 5x + 12$$
$$2.5x - 20 = 5x$$
$$-20 = 2.5x$$
$$-8 = x$$

In Exercises 29–31, students should list three values in the given interval.

29. $x \le 3$

30. $x < 6$

31. $x \le 2$

32. $x \le 9$

33. Possible answers given.

a. $d = 15g$

b. 150 mi

c. About 16.7 gal

d. The value of m is the number of miles a bus travels on 1 gal of gasoline. The value of b is the number of miles covered on 0 gal of gas, which should be 0 mi.

34. Possible answers given.

a. As price goes up, some customers will decide it is too expensive and will not buy corn.

b. As price goes up, fewer people will buy the corn, so the farmers have a larger supply of leftover corn.

c. $d = 260 - 60p$

d. $\ell = 85p - 45$

e. The graph follows. The leftovers and demand are equal at the point of intersection. This happens at a price of just over $2. To find the answer symbolically, solve $260 - 60p = 90p - 50$. The solution is $2.07.

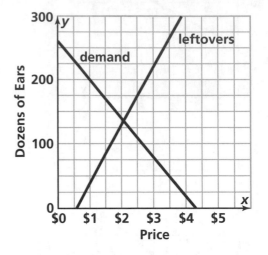

Note to the Teacher: Because models are approximations, the price here is also an approximation. In the table, the leftovers and demand are not shown as equal for a price of $2.

Connections

35. a. Linear; as x increases by 2 units, y increases by 1 unit.

b. Not linear; as x increases in 1-unit steps, y increases by increasing amounts.

c. Linear; for every 1-unit increase in x, y decreases by 1.

36. a. Linear; the rate of change is constant.

x	−5	−2	1	4
y	7	−2	−11	−20

b. Linear; the rate of change is constant.

x	−3	0	3	6
y	−34	−22	−10	2

c. Not linear; the rate of change is not constant.

x	−3	0	3	6
y	21	0	33	120

d. Linear; the rate of change is constant.

x	−3	0	3	10
y	13	4	−5	−26

37. $-5 < 3$

38. $\frac{2}{3} > \frac{1}{2}$

39. $\frac{9}{12} = \frac{3}{4}$

40. $3.009 < 3.1$

41. $\frac{-2}{3} < \frac{-1}{2}$

42. $-4.25 < 2.45$

43. $a = 1.5b$

44. -22 **45.** -22 **46.** 8

47. -8 **48.** -4 **49.** 4

50. -5 **51.** 8   **52.** 50

53. a. $\frac{-4}{-2} = 2 = 200\%$ and $1.5 = 150\%$.

b. 200% is the greatest; 60% is the least

54. a. Story 1 goes with Graph A. The first part of the graph shows height increasing rapidly as the plane ascends. The middle section shows height remaining constant as the plane holds its altitude. The last part shows height decreasing, rapidly at first and then more slowly, as the parachutist descends. The graph stops at a point just above the x-axis, where the parachutist got caught in the tree. The x-axis label could be "Time," and the y-axis label could be "Height."

Story 2 goes with Graph D. The graph shows the account balance increasing, slowly at first, and then more rapidly as time passes. The last section of the graph shows the balance dropping to half the amount, without any time passing, as half the money is removed. The x-axis label could be "Time," and the y-axis label could be "Account Balance."

Story 3 goes with Graph B. The graph shows the volume of the pile of gravel decreasing rapidly at first, and then less rapidly. Gerry removes half of the pile each day, but because the pile is smaller every day, the amount he removes is less and less every

day. The x-axis label could be "Day," and the y-axis label could be "Volume of Gravel."

b. Possible story: Graph C shows how a student travels during an afternoon. First he runs from his home to a friend's house at a constant speed, until he gets tired and walks. He meets his friend, and they travel back to his home in a car, gradually accelerating.

55. a. 2 in.   **b.** 2   **c.** $\frac{1}{2}$

d. They are reciprocals.

Extensions

56. a. $24,000; $42,000; $78,000

b. $B = (5,000 + 150L) + 0.20(5,000 + 150L)$ or $B = 6,000 + 180L$

c. $33,000, $60,000, $87,000

d. $B = (5,000 + 150L) + 0.15(5,000 + 150L)$ or $B = 5,750 + 172.5L$

57. a. $r = \ell + (\ell - 1) + 2\ell$, $r = 4(\ell - 1) + 3$, and $r = 4\ell - 1$

b. Possible explanations:

$r = \ell + (\ell - 1) + 2\ell$: There are ℓ rods along the bottom, $\ell - 1$ rods along the top, and 2 additional diagonal rods for every foot.

$r = 4(\ell - 1) + 3$: We start with 3 rods and then add 4 for each additional foot.

$r = 4\ell - 1$: Look at each 1-foot segment, except the last, as a triangle with a rod extending from the top like the one below. The last foot does not require the top segment, so we need to subtract one.

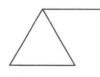

58. $r = n^2 + 3n$, $r = n(n + 3)$, and $r = (n + 3)n$

59. 6   **60.** D   **61.** H

62. a. Sid's formula will not work because it does not account for the fact that the cost for the first 10 min is fixed at $5.

b. Tina's formula works for any time beyond 10 min, but it does not work for times under 10 min.

c. Yes.

63. a. The Bluebird Taxi rule has two parts. For distances less than 2 mi, $f = 1.50$; for distances of 2 mi or more, $f = 1.2(d - 2) + 1.5$, because d is the distance in mi and f is the fare.

b. The parking charge rule needs two parts—one for times of 30 min or less and one for times greater than 30 min (or 0.5 hr). Furthermore, the way these charge schemes usually work, the charge for any time between 0.5 hr and 1.5 hr will be $2. Then the charge for any time between 1.5 hr and 2.5 hr will be $4, and so on. This is hard to express as a simple algebraic rule, but one could use $p = 2(t - 0.5)$, where p is price and t is time, and then round the result up to the nearest $2. For example, if $t = 4.7, p = 2(4.7 - 0.5) = 2(4.2) = 8.4$, which would round up to $10.

c. $p = 6.50n - 750$, where p is the profit in dollars and n is the number of tickets sold.

d. $c = 50 + 50t$, where t is the repair time required and c is the cost for the repair.

Possible Answers to Mathematical Reflections

1. A model allows you to summarize the overall trend in the data with a simple line or equation, and it lets you predict data values between and beyond the data points.

2. a. Figure out which variable is the independent variable and which is the dependent variable. Then find the rate of change in the dependent variable as the independent variable changes by a fixed amount. This is the slope m. Then you need to find the starting value, or the value of the dependent variable when the independent variable is 0. This is the y-intercept b. Plug the values of m and b into the equation $y = mx + b$.

b. Figure out the rate of change. This is the slope m. You can find the rate by dividing the difference in two y-values by the difference in the corresponding two x-values. Find the y-intercept b. If this is not a value in the table, use the rate of change to extend

the table to include a value for which the independent variable is 0. Plug the values of m and b into the equation $y = mx + b$.

c. Pick any two points on the line and use their coordinates to calculate the slope m. You do this by finding the ratio of differences in y-values to differences in the corresponding x-values, or $m = \frac{y_2 - y_1}{x_2 - x_1}$. Estimate the y-intercept b of the graph. You can also find the value of b by working backward from a known point, using the slope, or you can use the coordinates of one known point (x_0, y_0) on the line and the slope you have calculated to solve $y_0 = mx_0 + b$ for b.

3. a. You can graph the equation for the associated line and use the graph to estimate the solution. For example, to solve $500 = 245 + 5x$, you graph $y = 245 + 5x$, and then find the point on the line with y-coordinate 500. The x-coordinate of that point is the solution.

If you have a graphing calculator, you can enter the equation for the associated line and trace a table or graph to find the solution.

To solve the equation symbolically, apply the same operation to both sides to get x by itself on one side. For example, to solve $500 = 245 + 5x$, subtract 245 from both sides to get $255 = 5x$, and then divide both sides by 5 to get $51 = x$.

b. You can graph the two associated equations and find the point where the graphs intersect. For example, to solve $500 + 3x = 245 + 5x$, graph $y = 500 + 3x$ and $y = 245 + 5x$. The x-coordinate of the point of intersection is the solution.

If you have a graphing calculator, you can enter the two equations and trace a table or graph to find the x-value of the point of intersection.

To solve the equation symbolically, apply the same operation to both sides to get x by itself on one side. For example, to solve $500 + 3x = 245 + 5x$, subtract 245 from both sides to get $255 + 3x = 5x$, then subtract $3x$ from both sides to get $255 = 2x$, and then divide both sides by 2 to get $127.5 = x$.

Investigation 3   Inverse Variation

Mathematical and Problem-Solving Goals

- Explore situations that can be modeled by inverse variation relationships
- Investigate the nature of inverse variation in familiar contexts
- Compare inverse variations with linear relationships

Summary of Problems

Problem 3.1   Rectangles With Fixed Area

Students are introduced to inverse variation as they examine the relationship between length and width for rectangles with a fixed area.

Problem 3.2   Bridging the Distance

Students examine two more examples of inverse variation: the relationship between bridge length and breaking weight and the relationship between speed and time for a fixed distance. Students also contrast inverse variations with linear relationships.

Problem 3.3   Average Cost

Students solve a problem involving a school trip with a fixed total cost. They examine the relationship between the number of students who go on the trip and the per-student cost. Here again, students compare inverse variations with linear relationships.

	Suggested Pacing	Materials for Students	Materials for Teachers	ACE Assignments
All	$5\frac{1}{2}$ days	Calculators; grid paper; colored pens, pencils or markers; blank transparencies and transparency markers (optional); chart paper and markers (optional); student notebooks	Blank transparencies and transparency markers	
3.1	$1\frac{1}{2}$ days		Transparencies 3.1A and 3.1B	1, 2, 12–26, 40
3.2	$1\frac{1}{2}$ days		Transparencies 3.2A and 3.2B	3–9, 27–31, 41–45
3.3	$1\frac{1}{2}$ days			10, 11, 32–39, 46–48
M.R	$\frac{1}{2}$ day			

3.1 Rectangles With Fixed Area

Goal

- Explore situations that can be modeled by inverse variation relationship

Launch 3.1

Begin with a quick review of the concept of area. Have students recall the formula for area of a rectangle, which they learned in the grade 6 unit *Covering and Surrounding*. Work a couple of examples if students need practice.

Suggested Questions Ask:

- *What is area?* (the number of square units that fit inside a figure)

- *How do you find the area of a rectangle?* (Multiply the length and the width.) *How can you write this as a formula?* ($A = \ell w$)

- *If you know the area of a rectangle, how can you find possible lengths and widths?* (You can find factors of the area.)

Challenge students to find the width of a rectangle given an area and a length.

- *I am thinking of a rectangle with an area of 100 square units. Its length is 8 units. What is its width?* (12.5 units)

- *How did you find this width?* (by dividing 100 by 8)

- *How does this relate to the formula for area of a rectangle?* (If the area is length times width, then width must be area divided by length.)

Introduce the context of the free lots of land in Roseville. Make sure students understand that the lots have a fixed area and that they must be rectangular.

Suggested Questions Discuss the Getting Ready question.

- *What are some possible dimensions for a rectangular lot with area 21,800 square feet?* (Possible answers: 50 ft × 436 ft; 100 ft × 218 ft)

Describe the problem to students. They will look for patterns relating length and width for rectangles of fixed area.

Have students work on the problem in pairs.

Explore 3.1

Listening to Students As you observe and interact with students, consider the following questions:

- Are students aware of the division they need to do?

- Can they generalize this division to write an equation?

- Do they expect the equation to fit in the familiar form $y = mx + b$?

- Do they see connections between the equation here and the equation for area of a rectangle?

Summarize 3.1

Suggested Questions Ask some questions about the relationships:

- *What do you notice about how width changes in this table?* (As length increases, width decreases.)

- *How much does width decrease for each 1-inch increase in the length?* (It changes. The amount of decrease for each 1-inch increase gets smaller as the length increases.)

- *Is the change in width predictable?* (At this time, students may predict only that the change will continue to get smaller.)

- *If I gave you a length, how would you find the width? For example, what is the width for a length of 15 inches?* (Divide the area by the length, so $24 \div 15 = 1.6$ inches.)

- *For rectangles with an area of 24 square inches, how could you write an equation that shows how the width depends on the length?* (Because you divide the area by the length to find the width, the equation is $w = \frac{24}{\ell}$, or $w = 24 \div \ell$. Students may also write $\ell w = 24$ or $\ell = \frac{24}{w}$. If so, discuss the fact that these equations are equivalent.)

- *Is this a linear relationship?* (no)

- *How can you tell?* (From the table, equal changes in length do not lead to equal changes in width. From the equation, it cannot be written as $y = mx + b$. From the graph, the points form a curve, not a line.)

- *How are the two graphs you made similar?* (They have the same shape.)

- *How would you describe this shape?* (Students should notice that the graph is a decreasing curve.)

- *Describe the pattern of change shown in the graph.* (As the length increases, the width decreases, but not in a linear way.)

- *How are the graphs different?* (They pass through different coordinates.)

- *Where would each graph cross the y-axis? In other words, what are the y-intercepts?* (There are no y-intercepts. For example, for the first graph, the y-intercept would correspond to a rectangle with an area of 24 sq. in. and length of 0 in. This is impossible.)

- *Where would each graph cross the x-axis?* (It doesn't. An x-intercept would represent a rectangle with a width of 0 but a positive area. This is not possible.)

This is the first time students have written equations to describe nonlinear relationships. Spend some time looking at how students found the equations. Make sure they understand how to write the equations.

- *How are the two equations you wrote alike?* (Both have the form $w = \frac{A}{\ell}$ where A is a number that is the area of the rectangle.)

- *How are they different?* (The number A is different.)

- *Looking at the equation, how can you predict that the width will decrease as the length increases?* (You are dividing the area by the length. When you divide by a greater and greater number, the quotient gets smaller and smaller.)

Discuss other forms of the equation.

- *What is another way to write this equation?* ($A = \ell w$ or $\ell = \frac{A}{w}$)

Explain that all three equations are equivalent. You might ask students to explain how to get from one equation to another. For example, you can start with $w = \frac{A}{\ell}$ and multiply both sides by ℓ to get $\ell w = A$. Or, you can start with $A = \ell w$ and divide both sides by w to get $\frac{A}{w} = \ell$.)

You might wrap up the discussion by revisiting the bridge-length data students collected in Problem 1.2.

Suggested Question

- *How does the data from the bridge length experiment compare with the* (length, width) *data for rectangles with a fixed area?* (Both sets of data show a nonlinear, decreasing pattern of change.)

INVESTIGATION 3

3.1 Rectangles With Fixed Area

Mathematical Goal

- Explore situations that can be modeled by inverse variation relationships

Launch

Review the concept of area and the formula for area of a rectangle.

- *What is area?*
- *How do you find the area of a rectangle?*
- *I am thinking of a rectangle with an area of 100 square units. Its length is 8 units. What is its width?*
- *How did you find this width?*
- *How does this relate to the formula for area of a rectangle?*

Introduce the context of the free lots of land in Roseville. Discuss the Getting Ready question.

Describe the problem to students and have them work in pairs.

Materials
- Transparencies 3.1A and 3.1B
- Grid paper
- Transparencies and transparency markers

Explore

Listen to how students are thinking about the relationship between length and width. Are they aware of the division they need to do? Can they generalize this division to write an equation? Do they see connections between the equation here and the one for area of a rectangle?

Summarize

- *What do you notice about how width changes in this table?*
- *How much does width decrease for each 1-inch increase in the length?*
- *Is the change in width predictable?*
- *If I gave you a length, how would you find the width? For example, what is the width for a length of 15 inches?*
- *For rectangles with an area of 24 square inches, how could you write an equation that shows how the width depends on the length?*
- *Is this a linear relationship? How can you tell?*
- *How are the two graphs you made similar?*
- *Describe the pattern of change shown in the graph.*
- *How are the graphs different?*
- *Where would each graph cross the y-axis?*
- *Where would each graph cross the x-axis?*
- *How are the two equations you wrote alike? How are they different?*

Materials
- Student notebooks

continued on next page

continued

• *Looking at the equation, how can you predict the width will decrease as the length increases?*

• *What is another way to write this equation?*

Explain that the different forms are equivalent. Ask students to explain how to get from one form to another.

ACE Assignment Guide for Problem 3.1

Differentiated Instruction
Solutions for All Learners

Core 1, 2, 12
Other *Connections* 13–26; *Extensions* 40; unassigned choices from previous problems

Adapted For suggestions about adapting ACE exercises, see the *CMP Special Needs Handbook*.
Connecting to Prior Units 12: *Moving Straight Ahead, Covering and Surrounding*; 13–18: *Accentuate the Negative*

Answers to Problem 3.1

A. 1. (Figure 1)

2. **Rectangles With an Area of 24 in.²**

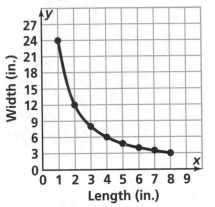

Length (in.)

3. As length increases, width decreases. The graph also decreases at a decreasing rate, so it is curved. The relationship is not linear.

4. $w = \frac{24}{\ell}$. Students may also write $\ell w = 24$ or $\ell = \frac{24}{w}$.

B. 1. $w = \frac{32}{\ell}$. Students may also write $\ell w = 32$ or $\ell = \frac{32}{w}$.

2. **Rectangles With an Area of 32 in.²**

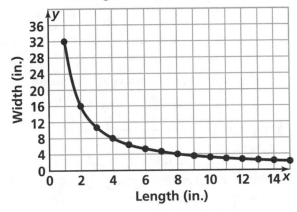

Length (in.)

C. Both can be written in the form $w = \frac{A}{\ell}$, where A is a fixed number. In one equation, $A = 24$, and in the other, $A = 32$.

D. The graphs are both decreasing curves, but they pass through different points.

Figure 1   **Rectangles With an Area of 24 in.²**

Length (in.)	1	2	3	4	5	6	7	8
Width (in.)	24	12	8	6	$\frac{24}{5}$	4	$\frac{24}{7}$	3

Goals

- Explore situations that can be modeled by inverse variation relationships

- Investigate the nature of inverse variation in familiar contexts

- Compare inverse variations with linear relationships

Students are familiar with the relationship between distance and time for travel at a fixed rate. In *Moving Straight Ahead,* students found their own walking rates and saw how distance changed as time increased. This is a linear relationship. In this problem, distance is fixed, and they see how rate varies with time.

Launch 3.2

This problem brings students from their intuitive work in Problem 3.1 to more sophisticated work, while introducing formal notation and language used with inverse variation.

- *The relationships you found between length and width for rectangles with an area of 24 in.^{2} and with an area of 32 in.^{2} are examples of an important type of nonlinear pattern called an inverse variation.*

Introduce the formal definition of inverse variation:

The relationship between two variables, x and y, is an inverse variation if $y = \frac{k}{x}$, or $xy = k$, where k is a constant that is not 0.

Write the two forms of the equation on the board or overhead.

Suggested Question

- *How are these two equations related?* (They are equivalent. We could get the second from the first by multiplying both sides by x. Or students may notice that these equations are part of the same fact family; saying $xy = k$ is the same as saying $y = k \div x$ or $y = \frac{k}{x}$.)

Point out that for any inverse variation relationship, the product of every pair of x and y

values is the same value, k. This is easy to see from the equation $xy = k$.

Revisit the inverse-variation equations students wrote in Problem 3.1. Ask students to identify the values of k in those equations.

Remind students about the bridge-length experiment in Problem 1.2. Remind them that the data in that experiment were not linear. Display the data and graph from the student book, which appear on Transparency 3.2A.

Suggested Questions

- *Here is the bridge-length data one group of students collected. Is this the graph of a linear relationship?* (no)

- *How do you know?* (It's not a straight line.)

- *Look at the table of data. Do you see any relationships or patterns?* (As length increases, the breaking weight decreases in a nonlinear pattern.)

Work with students to multiply the numbers in each (*bridge length, breaking weight*) pair. Write each product next to the corresponding row of the table.

- *Do you notice any patterns when we multiply each pair of values?* (The products are nearly the same.)

Discuss the first Getting Ready question.

- *Describe a curve that models the pattern in the data.* (Invite a student to the overhead to sketch a curve.)

Give students a few minutes to work in pairs to answer the rest of the questions in the Getting Ready. Then discuss their answers.

- *What value of k could you use to model these data with an inverse variation equation?* (Answers will vary slightly. The average of the products, 155, is a reasonable value for k.)

- *Write the equation.* ($y = \frac{155}{x}$, or $xy = 155$)

- *In your equation, why does the value of y decrease as the value of x increases?* (The variable x is in the denominator and increasing the denominator will make the fraction $\frac{155}{x}$ smaller.)

- *What happens to the value of* y *as the value of* x *gets close to 0? Why is that a reasonable pattern for the bridge experiment?* (As x gets close to 0, y gets very big. This is reasonable because shorter bridges are stronger.)

Move on to Problem 3.2. Remind students of a linear relationship with which they are already familiar: the relationship between distance and time for travel at a fixed speed.

Suggested Questions

- *If you are on a car trip and driving at 60 mph, what two variables might you be interested in?* (time and distance)

- *What equation relates time and distance?* ($d = 60t$, where d is distance in miles and t is time in hours)

- *Is this a linear relationship?* (yes)

- *How do you know?* (Possible answer: The equation fits the form $y = mx + b$; we have seen graphs of similar relationships, and these graphs were straight lines; the table would show an increase of 60 miles for every 1-hour increase in time.)

Tell students that you want them to think about a slightly different question.

- *Suppose you are going on a car trip of 60 miles. How long will the trip take if you travel at 60 mph?* (1 hour)

- *What if you travel more slowly, at 30 mph?* (It would take 2 hours.)

- *In this problem, you are going to consider what happens if the distance, rather than the rate, is fixed. The variables will be rate and time instead of distance and time.*

Have students work in pairs or groups of three.

(**Explore** 3.2)

As you circulate, make sure students understand that in Questions A and B, the distance is fixed. Time and average speed are changing. If you see students struggling, ask questions that point their attention to this idea, and remind them of the differences between these problems and the more familiar linear relationship in which speed is fixed.

Make sure all students can explain why the relationships in Questions A and B are inverse variations. Even students who are struggling with the ideas should be able to point to the shape of the graphs as justification. Most students should recognize the form of the equation by this point. If this is not the case, you will want to spend time in the summary with this idea.

(**Summarize** 3.2)

Spend some time with students discussing how they found the equations in Questions A, B, and C. Make sure they understand how to write the equations.

- *How are the equations you found in Questions A and B different from the equation you found in Question C?* (The equation in Question C is linear; the other two are not.)

- *What do we know about the relationships among time, speed, and distance?* [There are different ways to think about it: Distance equals speed times time ($d = st$), speed equals distance divided by time ($s = \frac{d}{t}$), and time equals distance divided by speed ($t = \frac{d}{s}$).]

- *What are some differences in the graphs, tables, and equations of linear relationships and those of inverse variations?* (The graph of a linear relationship is a straight line, which may be increasing or decreasing. The graph of an inverse variation is a decreasing curve. The table for a linear relationship shows a constant rate of change. For an inverse variation, the rate of change is not constant; the y-values decrease at a decreasing rate as x increases. The equation for a linear relationship can be written in the form $y = mx + b$. The equation for an inverse variation can be written as $y = \frac{k}{x}$.)

3.2

Bridging the Distance

Mathematical Goals

- Explore situations that can be modeled by inverse variation relationships
- Investigate the nature of inverse variation in familiar contexts
- Compare inverse variations with linear relationships

Launch

Introduce inverse variations. Relate the equations from the last problem to the general equations and have students identify the values of *k*.

Remind students of the Problem 1.2 experiment. Display Transparency 3.2A.

- *Is this the graph of a linear relationship? How do you know?*
- *Look at the table of data. Do you see any relationships or patterns?*
- *Do you notice any patterns when we multiply each pair of values?*

Have students work on the Getting Ready questions, and then discuss them.

Introduce the context of Problem 3.2.

- *If you are on a car trip and driving at 60 mph, what two variables might you be interested in? What equation relates time and distance?*
- *Is this a linear relationship? How do you know?*
- *Suppose you are going on a car trip of 60 miles. How long will the trip take if you travel at 60 mph? What if you travel more slowly, at 30 mph?*
- *In this problem, you are going to consider what happens if the distance, rather than the rate, is fixed. The variables will be rate and time instead of distance and time.*

The class can work in pairs or groups of three.

Materials

- Transparencies 3.2A and 3.2B
- Transparencies and transparency markers
- Grid paper

Explore

As you circulate, make sure students understand that in Questions A and B, the distance is fixed. Time and average speed are changing.

Make sure all students can explain why this relationship is an inverse variation.

Summarize

- *How are the equations you found in Questions A and B different from the equation you found in Question C?*
- *What do we know about the relationships among time, speed, and distance?*
- *What are some differences in the graphs, tables, and equations of linear relationships and those of inverse variations?*

Materials

- Student notebooks

Vocabulary

- inverse variation

ACE Assignment Guide for Problem 3.2

Differentiated Instruction
Solutions for All Learners

Core 3–9, 28
Other *Connections* 27, 29–31; *Extensions* 41–45; unassigned choices from previous problems

Adapted For suggestions about adapting ACE exercises, see the *CMP Special Needs Handbook*
Connecting to Prior Units 27–28: *Data About Us*; 30–31: *Moving Straight Ahead*

Answers to Problem 3.2

A. 1.

Cordova's Baltimore Trips

Time (h)	1.5	10	14	4	18
Average Speed (mi/h)	333.3	50	35.71	125	27.78

2. Curves will vary. This graph includes the points added in part (5).

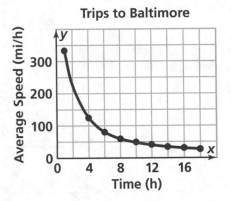

Trips to Baltimore

As trip time increases, average speed decreases at a decreasing rate, causing a curved pattern of points. This is an inverse variation pattern.

3. $s = \frac{500}{t}$ (or $st = 500$ or $t = \frac{500}{s}$)

4. 6 hr: 83.33 mph; 8 hr: 62.5 mph; 12 hr: 41.67 mph; 16 hr: 31.25 mph

5. See the graph for the points. Fit will vary.

B. 1. 300 mi. Multiply the average speed by the trip time for any average speed.

2. $t = \frac{300}{s}$ (or $s = \frac{300}{t}$ or $st = 300$)

3. As average speed increases, travel time decreases at a decreasing rate, forming a curve. In the equation $t = \frac{300}{s}$, we are dividing by s, and as the divisor s increases, the quotient t decreases.

4. 6.67 hr (or 6 hr 40 min) and 4.61 hr (or 4 hr 37 min)

C. 1.

Trip to Mackinac Island

Travel Time (h)	0	1	2	3	4	5	6
Distance (mi)	0	50	100	150	200	250	300

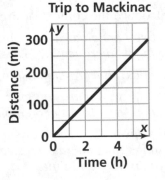

Trip to Mackinac

2. $d = 50t$

3. The distance changes in an increasing linear pattern. The constant rate of change is 50 mph.

4. The (*time, distance*) relationship has a straight-line graph and an equation of the form $y = mx + b$. The other relationships are inverse variations. Their graphs are decreasing curves, and their equations are of the form $y = \frac{k}{x}$.

3.3 Average Cost

Goals

- Explore situations that can be modeled by inverse variation relationships

- Investigate the nature of inverse variation in familiar contexts

- Compare inverse variations with linear relationships

Students see that, in an inverse variation, doubling the independent variable halves the dependent variable. Again, they compare what they have learned about inverse relationships with what they know about linear relationships.

Launch 3.3

One teacher launched this problem by telling a story about his childhood.

- *Have any of you ever split the cost of something with someone?*

- *When I was a child, my sister and I wanted the same album. Neither one of us had enough to buy it, so we split the cost. I paid half and she paid half. If there had been a third child in our family, we could have each paid even less. Even though the price of the record was the same, we each paid less by splitting the cost.*

- *In this problem, we will look at a similar story. There is something with a fixed cost that is being shared among several people.*

Read the problem scenario with students. This problem is similar enough to Problem 3.2 that students should not need much introduction to get started. Arrange students in pairs to work on the problem.

Explore 3.3

If students are having trouble writing an equation for Question A, encourage them to first make a table of (*number of students, per-student cost*) values.

Help students understand the purpose of Question C. The idea is that when we double the value of the independent variable in an inverse

variation, the value of the dependent variable is halved. This contrasts with linear relationships of the form $y = mx$, where doubling the independent variable (x) results in a doubling of the dependent variable (y). Without understanding this purpose, students might see Question C as needless repetition of Question B.

Note to the Teacher It is not always true in a linear relationship that, if you double the x-value, the y-value also doubles. For example, consider $y = 2x + 5$. If $x = 7$, then $y = 19$. If $x = 14$, then $y = 33$, which is not equal to 19×2. If a linear relationship is of the form $y = mx + 0$, then doubling the x-value will result in a doubled y-value. These relationships are sometimes called *proportional* for this quality.

Summarize 3.3

Talk with students about the answers to Questions A and B.

Suggested Questions About Question C, ask:

- *What happens to the per-student cost when the number of students doubles from 20 to 40?* (The per-student cost is halved. The cost per student when 20 students go is $37.50. If 40 students go, the cost per student would be $18.75.) *When the number of students doubles from 40 to 80?* (It's halved again.)

- *Why does it make sense that the per-student cost is halved when the number of students doubles?* (If you spread the cost among twice as many people, each person pays half as much.)

- *How can we see this pattern from the equation?* (The equation is $c = \frac{750}{n}$. Because n is in the denominator of $\frac{750}{n}$, if n is doubled, c is halved. For example, if we divide $\frac{750}{20}$, we will get half of what we get when we divide $\frac{750}{10}$.)

- *What would happen if we tripled the number of students?* (The cost per student would be $\frac{1}{3}$ as much. The cost per student when 20 students go is $37.50, so the cost per student if 60 students go is $\frac{1}{3}$ of $37.50, which is $12.50.)

INVESTIGATION 3

- *What is the relationship among cost per student (c), number of students (n), and total cost (T)?*

$(c = \frac{T}{n}, n = \frac{T}{c}$, or $T = cn)$

- *How are the relationships from Problem 3.3 alike and different from those in Problem 3.2?* (All are inverse variations. All have equations of the form $y = \frac{k}{x}$, or $xy = k$, where k is a constant whose value is determined by the specific relationship. Both have graphs that are decreasing curves.)

On the board, write $y = 12x$ and $xy = 12$.

- *Would the graphs of these two equations be the same?* (No; the graph of $y = 12x$ is an increasing line, while the graph of $xy = 12$ is a decreasing curve.)

You might use Question D to wrap up the discussion. It presents a linear relationship using the context of the class trip.

Have students formally identify the characteristics of a linear relationship and the characteristics of an inverse variation.

- *How are linear relationships different from inverse variations? How are they alike?* [In a linear relationship, the rate of change is constant. In an inverse variation, the rate of change decreases as the values of the independent variable increase. The graph of a linear relationship is a straight line (increasing or decreasing). The graph of an inverse relationship is a decreasing curve. An equation for a linear relationship can be written in the form $y = mx + b$, while the equation for an inverse variation can be written as $y = \frac{k}{x}$, or $xy = k$.]

3.3 Average Cost

PACING $1\frac{1}{2}$ days

Mathematical Goals

- Explore situations that can be modeled by inverse variation relationships
- Investigate the nature of inverse variation in familiar contexts
- Compare inverse variations with linear relationships

Launch

One teacher launched this problem by telling a story about his childhood.

- *Have any of you ever split the cost of something with someone?*

- *When I was a child, my sister and I wanted the same album. Neither one of us had enough to buy it, so we split the cost. I paid half and she paid half. If there had been a third child in our family, we could have each paid even less. Even though the price of the record was the same, we each paid less by splitting the cost.*

- *In this problem, we will look at a similar story. There is something with a fixed cost that is being shared among several people.*

Read the problem scenario with students. Students can work in pairs.

Materials
- Grid paper
- Transparencies and transparency markers

Explore

If students are having trouble writing an equation for Question A, encourage them to first make a table of values.

Help students understand the purpose of Question C. The idea is that when we double the value of the independent variable in an inverse relationship, the value of the dependent variable is halved. This contrasts with linear relationships of the form $y = mx$, where doubling the independent variable (x) results in a doubling of the dependent variable (y).

Summarize

Talk with students about the answers to Questions A and B. About Question C, ask:

- *What happens to the per-student cost when the number of students doubles from 20 to 40? When the number of students doubles from 40 to 80?*

- *Why does it make sense that the per-student cost is halved when the number of students doubles?*

- *How can we see this pattern from the equation?*

- *What would happen if we tripled the number of students?*

- *What is the relationship among cost per student, number of students, and total cost?*

- *How is the relationship between number of students and per-student cost for a fixed total cost similar to the relationship between average speed and time for a fixed distance?*

Materials
- Student notebooks

continued on next page

Summarize
continued

On the board, write $y = 12x$ and $xy = 12$.

- *Would the graphs of these two equations be the same?*

Use Question D to wrap up the discussion.

Have students formally identify the characteristics of a linear relationship and the characteristics of an inverse variation.

ACE Assignment Guide for Problem 3.3

Differentiated Instruction
Solutions for All Learners

Core 10, 11
Other *Connections* 32–39; *Extensions* 46–48; unassigned choices from previous problems

Adapted For suggestions about adapting ACE Exercise 11, see the *CMP Special Needs Handbook*.
Connecting to Prior Units 32–35: *Moving Straight Ahead*; 36–39: *Comparing and Scaling*

Answers to Problem 3.3

A. 1. $c = \frac{750}{n}$ (or $n = \frac{750}{c}$ or $cn = 750$)

2.

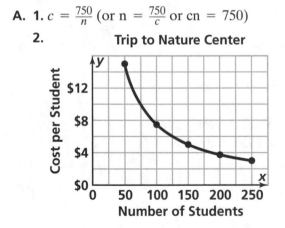

Trip to Nature Center

B. 1. a. Per-student cost decreases by $37.50, from $75 to $37.50.

b. Per-student cost decreases by about $0.68, from $7.50 to about $6.82.

c. Per-student cost decreases by about $0.18, from $3.75 to about $3.57.

2. The rate of change is not constant. In each part, the number of students increased by 10, but the decrease in per-student cost was not the same. The decrease got smaller each time.

C. 1. a. Per-student cost is halved, from $37.50 to $18.75.

b. Per-student cost is halved, from $18.75 to about $9.38.

c. Per-student cost is halved, from $9.37 to about $4.69. This is a decrease by half.

2. Doubling the number of students halves the per-student cost. Possible explanation: In the equation, $c = \frac{750}{n}$, doubling the number of students multiplies the denominator by 2. That's the same as multiplying the whole fraction, which represents the cost, by $\frac{1}{2}$.

D. 1. $a = 5n$

2.

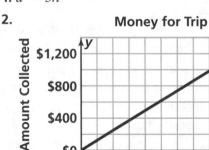

Money for Trip

3. This is a linear relationship. As n increases by 1 student, a increases by $5. The graph is a straight line.

Inverse Variation

In Investigation 1, you discovered that the relationship between bridge thickness and bridge strength is approximately linear. You also found that the relationship between bridge length and bridge strength is not linear. In this investigation, you will explore other nonlinear relationships.

3.1 Rectangles With Fixed Area

In recent years, the populations of many small towns have declined as residents move to large cities for jobs. The town of Roseville has developed a plan to attract new residents. The town is offering free lots of land to "homesteaders" who are willing to build houses. Each lot is rectangular and has an area of 21,800 square feet. The lengths and widths of the lots vary.

Getting Ready for Problem 3.1

- What are some possible dimensions for a rectangular lot with an area of 21,800 square feet?

In Problem 3.1, you will look at patterns in length and width values for rectangles with fixed area.

Investigation 3 Inverse Variation   **47**

Notes _____

_____

_____

Problem 3.1 Relating Length and Width

A. 1. Copy and complete this table.

Rectangles With Area 24 in.²

Length (in.)	1	2	3	4	5	6	7	8
Width (in.)	■	■	■	■	■	■	■	■

2. Plot your data on a grid like the one below. Then, draw a line or curve that seems to model the pattern in the data.

Rectangles With Area 24 in.²

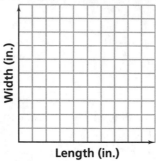

Length (in.)

3. Describe the pattern of change in the width as the length increases. Is the relationship between length and width linear?

4. Write an equation that shows how the width w depends on the length ℓ for rectangles with an area of 24 square inches.

B. Now consider rectangles with an area of 32 square inches.

1. Write an equation for the relationship between the length ℓ and the width w.

2. Graph your equation. Show lengths from 1 to 15 inches.

C. Compare your equations. How are they similar? How are they different?

D. Compare your graphs. How are they similar? How are they different?

ACE Homework starts on page 53.

Notes _____

_____

_____

_____

3.2 Bridging the Distance

The relationship between length and width for rectangles with a fixed area is not linear. It is an example of an important type of nonlinear pattern called an **inverse variation.**

The word "inverse" suggests that as one variable increases in value, the other variable decreases in value. However, the meaning of *inverse variation* is more specific than this. The relationship between two non-zero variables, x and y, is an inverse variation if

$$y = \frac{k}{x}, \text{ or } xy = k$$

where k is a constant that is not 0. The value of k is determined by the specific relationship.

> *How are the equations* $y = \frac{k}{x}$ *and* $xy = k$ *related?*

> *For the same* x-*value, will the two equations give different* y-*values?*

Inverse variation occurs in many situations. For example, consider the table and graph below. They show the (*bridge length, breaking weight*) data collected by a group of students.

Bridge Experiment Data

Length (in.)	Breaking Weight (pennies)
4	41
6	26
8	19
9	17
10	15

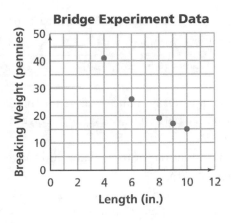

Bridge Experiment Data

Getting Ready for Problem 3.2

- Describe a curve that models the pattern in the data above.
- What value of k can you use to model these data with an inverse variation equation? Write the equation.
- In your equation, why does the value of y decrease as the value of x increases?
- What happens to the value of y as the value of x gets close to 0? Why is that a reasonable pattern for the bridge experiment?

Investigation 3 Inverse Variation **49**

Notes _____

_____

_____

_____

Mr. Cordova lives in Detroit, Michigan. He often travels to Baltimore, Maryland, to visit his grandfather. The trip is 500 miles each way. Here are his notes for his trips to Baltimore last year.

Date	Notes	Travel Time
February 15	Traveled by plane.	1.5 hours
May 22	Drove.	10 hours
July 3	Drove. Stopped for repairs.	14 hours
November 23	Flew. Flight delayed.	4 hours
December 23	Took overnight train.	18 hours

A. 1. Calculate the average speed in miles per hour for each trip. Record the results in a table like this.

Cordova's Baltimore Trips

Travel Time (hr)	■	■	■	■	■
Average Speed (mph)	■	■	■	■	■

2. Plot the data. Draw a line or curve that models the data pattern. Describe the pattern of change in average speed as travel time increases.

3. Write an equation for the relationship between travel time t and average speed s.

4. Use your equation to find the average speed for 500-mile trips that take 6 hours, 8 hours, 12 hours, and 16 hours.

5. Add the (*travel time, average speed*) data from part (4) to your graph. Do the new points fit the graph model you sketched for the original data?

Notes _____

_____

_____

_____

B. The Cordova family is planning a trip to Mackinac Island (mak uh naw) near the upper peninsula of Michigan. Mr. Cordova does some calculations to see how the travel time will change if the family drives at different average speeds.

Travel Times for Different Speeds

Average Speed (mi/h)	30	40	50	60	70
Travel Time (hr)	10	7.5	6	5	4.3

1. How far is it from Detroit to Mackinac Island?

2. What equation relates travel time *t* to average speed *s*?

3. Describe the pattern of change in the travel time as the average speed increases. How would that pattern appear in a graph of the data? How is it shown by your equation?

4. Predict the travel times if the Cordovas drive at average speeds of 45 miles per hour and 65 miles per hour.

C. Suppose Mr. Cordova decides to aim for an average speed of 50 miles per hour for the trip to Mackinac Island.

1. Make a table and graph to show how the distance traveled will increase as time passes. Show times from when the family leaves home to when they reach their destination.

2. Write an equation for the distance *d* the family travels in *t* hours.

3. Describe the pattern of change in the distance as time passes.

4. Compare the (*time, distance traveled*) graph and equation with the (*time, average speed*) graphs and equations in Questions A and B.

ACE Homework starts on page 53.

Notes _____

_____

_____

_____

3.3 Average Cost

The science teachers at Everett Middle School want to take their eighth-graders on an overnight field trip to a nature center. It costs $750 to rent the center facilities. The school budget does not provide funds to rent the nature center, so students must pay a fee. The trip will cost $3 per student if all 250 students go. However, the teachers know it is unlikely that all students can go. They want to find the cost per student for any number of students.

Problem 3.3 Inverse Variation Patterns

A. 1. Write an equation relating the cost c per student to the number of students n.

    2. Use your equation to make a graph showing how the cost per student changes as the number of students increases.

B. 1. Find the change in the cost per student as the number of students increases from

    a. 10 to 20   **b.** 100 to 110   **c.** 200 to 210

    2. How do your results show that the relationship between the number of students and the cost per student is not linear?

C. 1. Find the change in the per-student cost as the number of students increases from

    a. 20 to 40   **b.** 40 to 80   **c.** 80 to 160

    2. Describe the pattern in your results. Explain how your equation from Question A shows this pattern.

D. The science teachers decide to charge $5 per student for the trip. They will use any extra money to buy science equipment for the school.

    1. Write an equation for the amount a the teachers will collect if n students go on the trip.

    2. Sketch a graph of the relationship.

    3. Is this a linear relationship or an inverse variation? Explain.

ACE **Homework starts on page 53.**

52 Thinking With Mathematical Models

Notes _____

_____

_____

_____

Applications

1. Consider rectangles with an area of 16 square inches.

   a. Copy and complete the table.

   Rectangles With an Area of 16 in.²

Length (in.)	1	2	3	4	5	6	7	8
Width (in.)	▪	▪	▪	▪	▪	▪	▪	▪

   b. Make a graph of the data.

   c. Describe the pattern of change in width as length increases.

   d. Write an equation that shows how the width w depends on the length ℓ. Is the relationship linear?

2. Consider rectangles with an area of 20 square inches.

   a. Make a table of length and width data for at least five rectangles.

   b. Make a graph of your data.

   c. Write an equation that shows how the width w depends on the length ℓ. Is the relationship linear?

   d. Compare and contrast the graphs in this exercise and in Exercise 1.

   e. Compare and contrast the equations in this exercise and in Exercise 1.

3. A student collected these data from the bridge-length experiment.

   Bridge-Length Experiment

Length (in.)		4	6	8	9	10
Breaking Weight (pennies)		24	16	13	11	9

   a. Find an inverse variation equation that models these data.

   b. Explain how your equation shows that breaking weight decreases as length increases. Is this pattern reasonable for this situation? Explain.

Investigation 3 Inverse Variation   **53**

Notes _____

_____

_____

_____

For Exercises 4–7, tell whether the relationship between *x* and *y* is an inverse variation. If it is, write an equation for the relationship.

4.

x	1	2	3	4	5	6	7	8	9	10
y	10	9	8	7	6	5	4	3	2	1

5.

x	1	2	3	4	5	6	7	8	9	10
y	48	24	16	12	9.6	8	6.8	6	5.3	4.8

6.

x	2	3	5	8	10	15	20	25	30	40
y	50	33	20	12.5	10	6.7	5	4	3.3	2.5

7.

x	0	1	2	3	4	5	6	7	8	9
y	100	81	64	49	36	25	16	9	4	1

8. A marathon is a 26.2-mile race. The best marathon runners can complete the race in a little more than 2 hours.

a. Make a table and graph that show how the average running speed for a marathon changes as the time increases. Show times from 2 to 8 hours in 1-hour intervals.

b. Write an equation for the relationship between time *t* and average running speed *s* for a marathon.

c. Tell how the average running speed changes as the time increases from 2 hours to 3 hours. From 3 hours to 4 hours. From 4 hours to 5 hours.

d. How do the answers for part (c) show that the relationship between average running speed and time is not linear?

Notes _____

_____

_____

_____

9. On one day of a charity bike ride, the route covers 50 miles. Individual riders cover this distance at different average speeds.

   Homework Help Online
   PHSchool.com
   For: Help with Exercise 9
   Web Code: ape-1309

   a. Make a table and a graph that show how the riding time changes as the average speed increases. Show speed values from 4 to 20 miles per hour in intervals of 4 miles per hour.

   b. Write an equation for the relationship between the riding time t and average speed s.

   c. Tell how the riding time changes as the average speed increases from 4 to 8 miles per hour. From 8 to 12 miles per hour. From 12 to 16 miles per hour.

   d. How do the answers for part (c) show that the relationship between average speed and time is not linear?

10. Students in Mr. Einstein's science class complain about the length of his tests. He argues that a test with more questions is better for students because each question is worth fewer points. All of Mr. Einstein's tests are worth 100 points. Each question is worth the same number of points.

    a. Make a table and a graph that show how the number of points per question changes as the number of questions increases. Show point values for 2 to 20 questions in intervals of 2.

    b. Write an equation for the relationship between the number of questions n and the points per question p.

    c. Tell how the points per question changes as the number of questions increases from 2 to 4. From 4 to 6. From 6 to 8. From 8 to 10.

    d. How do the answers for part (c) show that the relationship between the number of questions and the points per question is not linear?

Notes _____

_____

_____

_____

11. Testers drive eight vehicles 200 miles on a test track at the same speed. The table shows the amount of fuel each vehicle uses.

Fuel-Efficiency Test

Vehicle Type	Fuel Used (gal)
Large Truck	20
Large SUV	18
Limousine	16
Large Sedan	12
Small Truck	10
Sports Car	12
Compact Car	7
Sub-Compact Car	5

a. Find the fuel efficiency in miles per gallon for each vehicle.

b. Make a graph of the (*fuel used, miles per gallon*) data. Describe the pattern of change shown in the graph.

c. Write a formula for calculating the fuel efficiency based on the fuel used for a 200-mile test drive.

d. Tell how the fuel efficiency changes as the amount of fuel used increases from 5 to 10 gallons. From 10 to 15 gallons. From 15 to 20 gallons.

e. How do the answers for part (d) show that the relationship between the fuel used and the fuel efficiency is not linear?

Connections

12. Suppose the town of Roseville is giving away lots with perimeters of 500 feet, rather than with areas of 21,800 square feet.

a. Copy and complete this table.

**Rectangles With a
Perimeter of 500 Feet**

Length (ft)	■	■	■	■	■
Width (ft)	■	■	■	■	■

56 Thinking With Mathematical Models

Notes _____

_____

_____

_____

b. Make a graph of the (*length, width*) data. Draw a line or curve that models the data pattern.

c. Describe the pattern of change in width as length increases.

d. Write an equation for the relationship between length and width. Is this a linear relationship? Explain.

A number b is the [additive inverse] of the number a if $a + b = 0$. For example, -5 is the additive inverse of 5 because $5 + (-5) = 0$. For Exercises 13–18, find the additive inverse of each number.

Go Online
PHSchool.com
For: Multiple-Choice Skills Practice
Web Code: apa-1354

13. 2

14. $-\frac{6}{2}$

15. 2.5

16. -2.11

17. $\frac{7}{3}$

18. $\frac{3}{7}$

19. On a number line, graph each number in Exercises 13–18 and its additive inverse. Describe any patterns you see.

A number b is the [multiplicative inverse] of the number a if $ab = 1$. For example, $\frac{3}{2}$ is the multiplicative inverse of $\frac{2}{3}$ because $\left(\frac{2}{3}\right)\left(\frac{3}{2}\right) = 1$. For Exercises 20–25, find the multiplicative inverse of each number.

20. 2

21. -2

22. 0.5

23. 4

24. $\frac{3}{4}$

25. $\frac{5}{3}$

26. On a number line, graph each number in Exercises 20–25 and its multiplicative inverse. Describe any patterns you see.

Jamar takes a 10-point history quiz each week. Here are his scores on the first five quizzes: 8, 9, 6, 7, 10. Use this information for Exercises 27–28.

27. Multiple Choice What is Jamar's average quiz score?

A. 6

B. 7

C. 8

D. 9

28. a. Jamar misses the next quiz and gets a 0. What is his average after six quizzes?

b. After 20 quizzes, Jamar's average is 8. He gets a 0 on the 21st quiz. What is his average after 21 quizzes?

c. Why did a score of 0 have a different effect on the average when it was the sixth score than when it was the 21st score?

Notes _____

_____

_____

_____

29. Suppose a car travels at a speed of 60 miles per hour. The equation $d = 60t$ represents the relationship between the time t in hours and the distance d driven in miles. This relationship is an example of a *direct variation*. A relationship between variables x and y is a direct variation if it can be expressed as $y = kx$, where k is a constant.

a. Find two relationships in this unit that are direct variations. Give the equation for each relationship.

b. For each relationship from part (a), find the ratio of the dependent variable to the independent variable. How is the ratio related to k in the general equation?

c. Suppose the relationship between x and y is a direct variation. How do y-values change as the x-values increase? How does this pattern of change appear in a graph of the relationship?

d. Compare direct variation and inverse variation. Be sure to discuss the graphs and equations for these types of relationships.

Solve the equation using a symbolic method. Then, describe how the solution can be found by using a graph and a table.

30. $5x - 28 = -3$ **31.** $10 - 3x = 7x - 10$

For Exercises 32–34, find the equation of the line with the given information.

32. slope $-\frac{1}{2}$, y-intercept $(0, 5)$

33. slope 3, passes through the point $(2, 2)$

34. passes through the points $(5, 2)$ and $(1, 10)$

35. Find the equation for the line below.

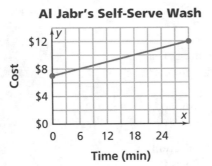

Al Jabr's Self-Serve Wash

36. Suppose 6 cans of tomato juice cost $3.20. Find the cost for

a. 1 can   **b.** 10 cans   **c.** n cans

Notes _____

_____

_____

_____

For Exercises 37–39, tell which store offers the better buy. Explain your choice.

37. *Gus's Groceries*: Tomatoes are 6 for $4.00
   Super Market: Tomatoes are 8 for $4.60

38. *Gus's Groceries*: Cucumbers are 4 for $1.75
   Super Market: Cucumbers are 5 for $2.00

39. *Gus's Groceries*: Apples are 6 for $3.00
   Super Market: Apples are 5 for $2.89

Extensions

40. This net folds up to make a rectangular prism.

   a. What is the volume of the prism?

   b. Suppose the dimensions of the shaded face are doubled. The other dimensions are adjusted so that the volume remains the same. What are the dimensions of the new prism?

   c. Which prism has the smaller surface area, the original prism or the prism from part (b)? Explain.

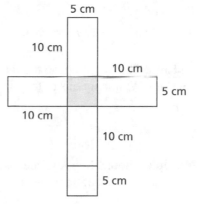

41. Ms. Singh drives 40 miles to her sister's house. Her average speed is 20 miles per hour. On her way home, her average speed is 40 miles per hour. What is her average speed for the round trip?

Investigation 3 Inverse Variation **59**

Notes

42. The drama club members at Henson Middle School are planning their spring show. They decide to charge $4.50 per ticket. They estimate their expenses for the show at $150.

   a. Write an equation for the relationship between the number of tickets sold and the club's total profit.

   b. Make a table to show how the profit changes as the ticket sales increase from 0 to 500 in intervals of 50.

   c. Make a graph of the (*tickets sold, total profit*) data.

   d. Add a column (or row) to your table to show the per-ticket profit for each number of tickets sold. For example, for 200 tickets, the total profit is $750, so the per-ticket profit is $750 ÷ 200, or $3.75.

   e. Make a graph of the (*tickets sold, per-ticket profit*) data.

   f. How are the patterns of change for the (*tickets sold, total profit*) data and (*tickets sold, per-ticket profit*) data similar? How are they different? How are the similarities and differences shown in the tables and graphs of each relationship?

For Exercises 43–45, find the value of *c* for which both ordered pairs satisfy the same inverse variation. Then, write an equation for the relationship.

43. $(3, 16), (12, c)$ **44.** $(3, 9), (4, c)$ **45.** $(3, 4), (4, c)$

46. Multiple Choice The force acting on a falling object due to gravity is related to the mass and acceleration of the object. For a fixed force *F*, the relationship between mass *m* and acceleration *a* is an inverse variation. Which equation shows the relationship between *F*, *m*, and *a*?

   A. $F = ma$ **B.** $m = Fa$ **C.** $\frac{m}{F} = a$ **D.** $\frac{m}{a} = F$

47. Multiple Choice Suppose the time *t* in the equation $d = rt$ is held constant. What happens to the distance *d* as the rate *r* increases?

   F. *d* decreases.   **G.** *d* increases.

   H. *d* stays constant.   **J.** There is not enough information.

48. Multiple Choice Suppose the distance *d* in the equation $d = rt$ is held constant. What happens to the time *t* as the rate *r* increases?

   A. *t* decreases.   **B.** *t* increases.

   C. *t* stays constant.   **D.** There is not enough information.

Notes _____

_____

_____

_____

Mathematical Reflections 3

In this investigation, you explored several examples of inverse variations and looked for patterns in the tables, graphs, and equations of these relationships. These questions will help you summarize what you have learned.

Think about your answers to these questions. Discuss your ideas with other students and your teacher. Then, write a summary of your findings in your notebook.

1. Suppose the relationship between variables x and y is an inverse variation.

   a. How do the values of y change as values of x increase?

   b. Describe the pattern in a graph of (x, y) values.

   c. Describe the equation that relates the values of x and y.

2. How is an inverse relationship similar to a linear relationship? How is it different?

Notes _____

_____

_____

_____

Investigation 3

ACE Assignment Choices

Problem 3.1
Core 1, 2, 12
Other *Connections* 13–19, 20–26; *Extensions* 40; unassigned choices from previous problems

Problem 3.2
Core 3–9, 28
Other *Connections* 27, 29–31; *Extensions* 41–45; unassigned choices from previous problems

Problem 3.3
Core 10, 11
Other *Connections* 32–39; *Extensions* 46–48; unassigned choices from previous problems

Adapted For suggestions about adapting ACE exercises, see the *CMP Special Needs Handbook*.
Connecting to Prior Units 12: *Moving Straight Ahead, Covering and Surrounding*; 13–18, 20–25: *Accentuate the Negative*; 27–28: *Data About Us*; 30–35: *Moving Straight Ahead*; 36–39: *Comparing and Scaling*

Applications

1. a. (Figure 2)
   b. **Rectangles With an Area of 16 in.²**

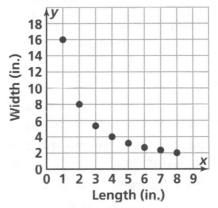

   c. As length increases, width decreases at a decreasing rate.
   d. $w = \frac{16}{\ell}$ (or $w\ell = 16$, or $\ell = \frac{16}{w}$); not linear

2. a. Values in table will vary. See Figure 3.

Figure 2 **Rectangles With an Area of 16 in.²**

Length (in.)	1	2	3	4	5	6	7	8
Width (in.)	16	8	$\frac{16}{3}$	4	$\frac{16}{5}$	$\frac{16}{6}$	$\frac{16}{7}$	2

Figure 3 **Rectangles With an Area of 20 in.²**

Length (in.)	1	2	3	4	5	6	7	8
Width (in.)	20	10	$\frac{20}{3}$	5	4	$\frac{10}{3}$	$\frac{20}{7}$	$\frac{5}{2}$

b. Points will vary.

Rectangles With an Area of 20 in.²

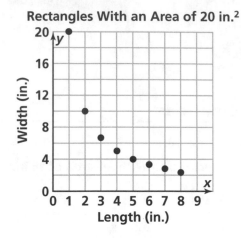

Length (in.)

c. $w = \frac{20}{\ell}$; not linear

d. The graphs are similar in shape, but the coordinates of the points are different.

e. The equations have the same form, but the constant is different.

3. a. Answers will vary, but $y = \frac{96}{x}$, where x is the length and y is the breaking weight, is a reasonable choice.

b. In the equation $y = \frac{96}{x}$, x (or length) is in the denominator, so, as x increases, y (or breaking weight) decreases. This is reasonable because the data show that as the length of a bridge increases, the strength decreases.

4. Not an inverse variation

5. Inverse variation; $y = \frac{48}{x}$

6. Inverse variation; $y = \frac{100}{x}$

7. Not an inverse variation

8. a.

Marathon Speeds

Time (h)	Running Speed (mi/h)
2	13.1
3	8.73
4	6.55
5	5.24
6	4.37
7	3.74
8	3.28

Marathon Speeds

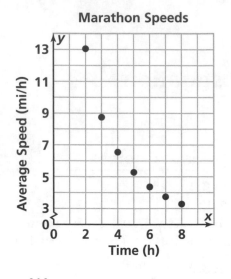

Time (h)

b. $s = \frac{26.2}{t}$

c. From 2–3 hr: decreases by 4.37 mph; from 3–4 hr: decreases by 2.18 mph; from 4–5 hr: decreases by 1.31 mph

d. For constant change in time, the change in average speed is not constant.

9. a.

Charity Bike Ride

Time (h)	Riding Speed (mi/h)
4	12.5
8	6.25
12	4.17
16	3.125
20	2.5

Charity Bike Ride

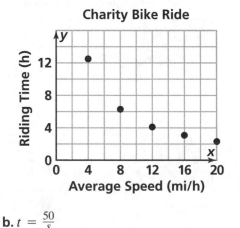

Average Speed (mi/h)

b. $t = \frac{50}{s}$

c. From 4–8 mph: decreases by 6.25 hours; from 8–12 mph: decreases by 2.08 hours; from 12–16 mph: decreases by 1.05 hours

d. For constant change in average riding speed, the change in time is not constant.

10. a.

Mr. Einstein's Tests

Number of Questions	Points per Question
2	50
4	25
6	16.67
8	12.5
10	10
12	8.33
14	7.14
16	6.25
18	5.56
20	5

Mr. Einstein's Tests

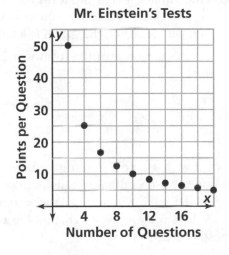

b. $p = \frac{100}{q}$

c. Decreases by 25 points per question; decreases by 8.32 points per question; decreases by 4.17 points per question; decreases by 2.5 points per question

d. For constant change in the number of questions, that change in points per question is not constant.

11. a.

Vehicle Type	Fuel Used (gal)	Fuel Efficiency (mi/gal)
Large Truck	20	10
Large SUV	18	11.11
Limousine	16	12.5
Large Sedan	12	16.67
Small Truck	10	20
Sports Car	12	16.67
Compact Car	7	28.57
Sub-Compact Car	5	40

b.

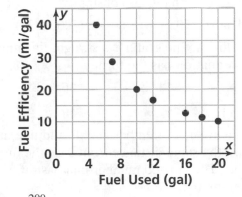

Fuel Efficiency

c. $e = \frac{200}{u}$

d. Decreases by 20 mpg; decreases by 6.67 mpg; decreases by 3.33 mpg

e. Constant change in fuel used does not lead to constant change in fuel efficiency.

Connections

12. a. Possible table:

Rectangles With a Perimeter of 500 ft

Length (ft)	50	100	150	200	225
Width (ft)	200	150	100	50	25

b.

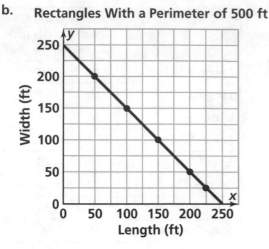

Rectangles With a Perimeter of 500 ft

(graph: Width (ft) vs Length (ft))

c. As length increases, width decreases. The rate of change is constant.

d. $w = 250 - \ell$ or $w = \frac{1}{2}(500 - 2\ell)$. This is linear. The graph is a straight line and the equation has the form $y = mx + b$.

13. –2   **14.** 3   **15.** –2.5

16. 2.11   **17.** $-\frac{7}{3}$ **18.** $-\frac{3}{7}$

19. (Figure 4); A number and its additive inverse are the same distance from 0 on the number line. The labeled number line has reflection symmetry.

20. $\frac{1}{2}$ **21.** $-\frac{1}{2}$

22. 2   **23.** $\frac{1}{4}$

24. $\frac{4}{3}$ **25.** $\frac{3}{5}$

26. (Figure 5); Numbers greater than 1 have multiplicative inverses between 0 and 1. Numbers less than –1 have multiplicative inverses between –1 and 0.

27. C

28. a. 6.7

  b. 7.62

  c. The effect was different because the relationship between number of quizzes and average quiz scores is not linear.

29. a. Possible answer: $y = 5x$ (ACE 19, Investigation 2) and $d = 50t$ (Problem 3.2 Question C). The ratio $\frac{y}{x}$ is 5 and the ratio $\frac{d}{t}$ is 50.

  b. The ratio equals k in both cases.

  c. Possible answer: y changes by k as x changes by 1. This pattern results in a straight-line graph with slope k.

  d. With a direct variation the graph is a line, and the equation is of the form $y = kx$ where the slope of the line equals k. With an inverse variation, the graph is a curve, and the equation is of the form $y = \frac{k}{x}$.

30. $x = 5$;
$$5x - 28 = -3$$
$$5x = 25$$
$$x = 5$$

To solve with a graph, graph $y = 5x - 28$, and find the x-coordinate of the point where $y = -3$. To solve with a table, make a table of (x, y) values for $y = 5x - 28$, find the x-value corresponding to $y = -3$.

Figure 4

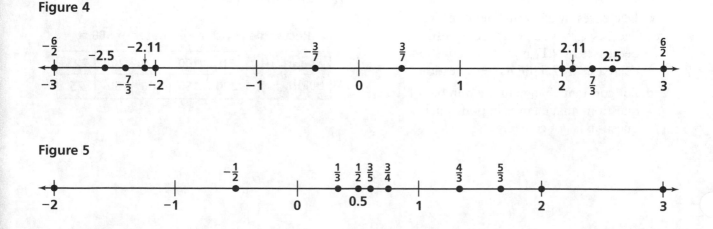

Figure 5

31. $x = 2$;

$$10 - 3x = 7x - 10$$
$$10 = 10x - 10$$
$$20 = 10x$$
$$x = 2$$

To solve with a graph, graph $y = 10 - 3x$, and $y = 7x - 10$, and find the x-coordinate of the intersection point. To solve with a table, make a table of (x, y) values for $y = 5x - 28$ and $y = 10 - 3x$, and find the x-value for which the y-values are the same.

32. $y = -\frac{1}{2}x + 5$

33. $y = 3x - 4$

34. $y = -2x + 12$

35. $y = \frac{1}{6}x + 7$. To find the slope, take the points $(30, 12)$ and $(6, 8)$ on the line and find the vertical change (4) and the horizontal change (24). Slope is the ratio $\frac{vertical\ change}{horizontal\ change} = \frac{4}{24} = \frac{1}{6}$

36. a. About \$0.53; \$3.20 ÷ 6 ≈ 0.53.

   b. About \$5.30; 0.53 × 10 = 5.3

   c. 0.53n

37. Super Market; Super Market charges about \$0.58 per tomato and Gus's Groceries charges about \$0.67.

38. Super Market; Gus's Groceries charges about \$0.44 per cucumber and Super Market charges \$0.40.

39. Gus's Groceries; Gus's Groceries charges \$0.50 per apple and Super Market charges about \$0.58.

Extensions

40. a. 250 cm³

   b. 10 cm by 10 cm by 2.5 cm

   c. The surface area of the original prism is 250 cm². The surface area of the prism in part (b) is 300 cm². The surface area of the original prism is smaller.

41. Ms. Singh traveled 80 mi in 3 hr, for an average speed of 80/3 = 26.67 mph.

42. a. If x is the number of tickets sold and y is the profit, then $y = 4.5x - 150$.

b and d.

Spring Show Ticket Sales

Tickets Sold	Total Profit	Per-Ticket Profit
0	−150	—
50	\$75	\$1.50
100	\$300	\$3.00
150	\$525	\$3.50
200	\$750	\$3.75
250	\$975	\$3.90
300	\$1,200	\$4.00
350	\$1,425	\$4.07
400	\$1,650	\$4.13
450	\$1,875	\$4.17
500	\$2,100	\$4.20

c.

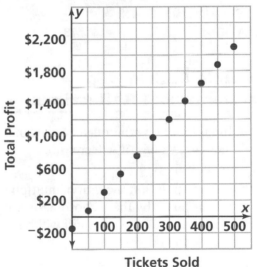

Spring Show Ticket Sales

d. See table above.

e.

Spring Show Ticket Sales

f. The pattern for total profit is linear; the pattern for per-ticket profit is not. The graph for total profit is a straight line; the graph for per-ticket profit is a curve. In the column for total profit, there is a constant difference in values; in the per-ticket profit column, there is not. The per-ticket profit decreases by a smaller and smaller amount as the number of tickets sold increases.

43. $(3, 16), (12, 4)$; $y = \frac{48}{x}$

44. $(3, 9), (4, \frac{27}{4})$; $y = \frac{27}{x}$

45. $(3, 4), (4, 3)$; $y = \frac{12}{x}$

46. A   **47.** G   **48.** A

Possible Answers to Mathematical Reflections

1. a. In an inverse variation, as values of x increase, values of y decrease at a decreasing rate.

b. For any point on the graph, multiplying the x-coordinate by the y-coordinate will yield a constant value. The graph will be a decreasing curve.

c. $y = \frac{k}{x}, xy = k$, or $x = \frac{k}{y}$.

2. In a linear relationship, the rate of change is constant. In an inverse variation, the rate of change decreases as the values of the independent variable increase. The graph of a linear relationship is a straight line (increasing or decreasing). The graph of an inverse relationship is a decreasing curve. An equation for a linear relationship can be written in the form $y = mx + b$, while the equation for an inverse variation can be written as $y = \frac{k}{x}$, or $xy = k$.

Answers to Looking Back and Looking Ahead

1. a. Line will vary.

Average Growth of Properly-Fed Pig

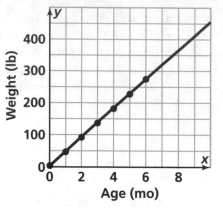

b. Possible equation: $y = 45x + 3$

c. Answers will vary. For the equation above, the slope m suggests that for every month, the weight increases by 45 lb. The y-intercept b suggests that the pig was 3 lb when it was born.

d. Answers will vary. The equation above predicts that at 3.5 mo, the pig weighed 160 lb. At 7 mo, the pig weighed roughly 318 lb.

2. a.   **Temperature and Food Eaten**

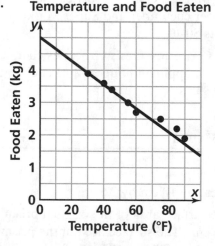

b. Possible equation: $y = -0.04x + 5$

c. Answers will vary. For the equation above, the slope m suggests that for every increase of 30°F in temperature, there is a decrease of 1 kg in food eaten. The y-intercept b suggests that the goat would eat 5 kg of food if the temperature were 0° F.

d. Answers will vary. The equation above predicts that, when it is 50°, the goat will eat 3 kg of food. When it is 70°, the goat will eat 2.2 kg of food.

Note to the Teacher Because the equation model is an approximation, the amount of food is also an approximation. The 2.2 kg of food eaten at 70°, calculated using the equation, does not fall between the amounts for 60° and 75° in the table. Students will develop methods for getting better lines of fit for their data in later mathematics courses.

3. a.

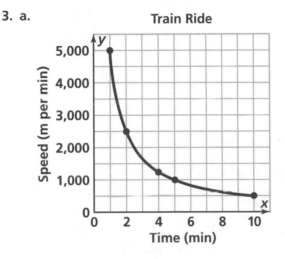

Train Ride

b. For times greater than 5 min, the speeds get more reasonable.

c. $5,000 = st$

d. The relationship is an inverse variation. As time increases, speed decreases, but it does not decrease at a constant rate. The product of the time and speed is always 5,000.

4. When the points on the graph fall in an approximately straight-line pattern or when there is a constant or near-constant rate of change, the data can be modeled by a linear equation in the form $y = mx + b$. The slope m shows the rate of change and the

y-intercept b generally shows a starting point (where $x = 0$).

5. The rate of change is not constant in an inverse variation, so the graph is curved. In a linear relationship, the graph is a straight line, indicating a constant rate of change. The equations for linear and inverse relationships are similar because both involve two variables, but a linear equation has one variable multiplied by a constant and an inverse variation equation involves multiplying two variables and setting them equal to a constant value. The linear equation also includes an additive constant in the equation—namely, the y-intercept. The inverse relationship has no y-intercept.

6. A graph model can be used to estimate values not given in the original data set. An equation model can be used to calculate values not in the data set. For practical problems, this means you will be able to predict what will happen between and beyond existing data values.

7. One limitation is that the data may not follow the pattern exactly, especially in extreme circumstances. For example, a goat will not eat an unlimited amount of food. The pattern may be approximately linear or approximately an inverse variation only for a restricted range of values.

Looking Back and Looking Ahead

Unit Review

While working on the problems in this unit, you extended your skill in writing equations to express linear relationships. You also learned about a type of nonlinear relationship called an inverse variation. You used inverse and linear relationships to solve problems and make predictions.

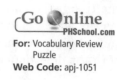

Go Online
PHSchool.com
For: Vocabulary Review Puzzle
Web Code: apj-1051

Use Your Understanding: Linear and Inverse Variation

Test your understanding of linear relationships and inverse variations by solving the following problems about a recreation area that has a playground, hiking trails, amusement rides, and a small farm.

1. This table shows the growth of one pig that was raised on the farm.

Average Growth of Properly Fed Pig

Age (mo)	0	1	2	3	4	5	6
Weight (lb)	3	48	92	137	182	228	273

SOURCE: Your 4-H Market Hog Project, Iowa State University.

a. Make a graph of the (*age, weight*) data. Draw a line that seems to fit the data pattern.

b. Find a linear equation in the form $y = mx + b$ for your line from part (a).

c. What do the values of m and b in your equation tell you about the growth of the pig?

d. Use your equation to estimate the pig's weight at 3.5 months and at 7 months.

Notes _____

_____

_____

_____

2. One group of students suspects that farm animals eat less when the weather is warmer. They ask the farm staff to keep a record of what an adult goat eats on days with different average temperatures.

Food Consumption for a Goat

Average Daily Temperature (°F)	30	40	45	55	60	75	85	90
Food Eaten (kg)	3.9	3.6	3.4	3.0	2.7	2.5	2.2	1.9

a. Make a graph of the (*temperature, food eaten*) data. Draw a line that seems to fit the data pattern.

b. Find a linear equation in the form $y = mx + b$ for your line from part (a).

c. What do the values of m and b tell you about the relationship between temperature and the goat's food consumption?

d. Use your equation to predict how much the goat would eat on a day with an average temperature of 50°F. On a day with an average temperature of 70°F.

3. A small train gives visitors rides around the park on a 5,000-meter track. The time the trip takes varies. When many people are waiting in line, the drivers go quickly. When there are fewer people waiting, they go more slowly.

a. Sketch a graph showing how the average speed (in meters per minute) changes as the trip time (in minutes) increases.

b. For what parts of your graph are the predicted speeds realistic? Explain.

c. Write an equation relating the average speed s to the trip time t.

d. Write several sentences explaining as accurately as possible how average speed changes as trip time changes. In particular, describe the type of variation involved in this relationship.

Looking Back and Looking Ahead   **63**

Notes _____

_____

_____

_____

Explain Your Reasoning

In this unit, you learned how to use models of linear relationships and inverse variations to solve a variety of problems. When you present work based on these relationships, you should be able to justify your calculations and conclusions.

4. How do you decide when a data pattern can be modeled well by a linear equation in the form $y = mx + b$? How will the values m and b relate to the data pattern?

5. How are the data patterns, graphs, and equations for the inverse variations you studied similar to and different from those modeled by linear equations?

6. How can a graph or equation model for a relationship be used to solve practical problems?

7. What limitations do mathematical models have as problem-solving tools?

Look Ahead

The work you did with linear relationships and inverse variations in this unit will be useful in many upcoming *Connected Mathematics* units and in the algebra and calculus courses you take in the future. As you progress through high school and college, you will see that linear and inverse relationships have applications in science, economics, business, technology, and many other fields of study.

Notes _____

_____

_____

_____

A

additive inverses Two numbers, a and b, that satisfy the equation $a + b = 0$. For example, 3 and -3 are additive inverses, and $\frac{1}{2}$ and $-\frac{1}{2}$ are additive inverses.

inversos aditivos Dos números, a y b, que cumplen con la ecuación $a + b = 0$. Por ejemplo, 3 y -3 son inversos aditivos, y $\frac{1}{2}$ y $-\frac{1}{2}$ son inversos aditivos.

I

inequality A statement that two quantities are not equal. The symbols $>$, $<$, $\geq$, and $\leq$ are used to express inequalities. For example, if a and b are two quantities, then "a is greater than b" is written as $a > b$, and "a is less than b" is written as $a < b$. The statement $a \geq b$ means "a is greater than or equal to b." The statement $a \leq b$ means that "a is less than or equal to b."

desigualdad Enunciado que dice que dos cantidades no son iguales. Los signos $>$, $<$, $\geq$, y $\leq$ se usan para expresar desigualdades. Por ejemplo, si a y b son dos cantidades, entonces "a es mayor que b", se escribe $a > b$, y "a es menor que b" se escribe $a < b$. El enunciado $a \geq b$ quiere decir "a es mayor que o igual a b." El enunciado $a \leq b$ quiere decir "a es menor que o igual a b."

inverse variation A nonlinear relationship in which the product of two variables is constant. An inverse variation can be represented by an equation of the form $y = \frac{k}{x}$, or $xy = k$, where k is a constant. In an inverse variation, the values of one variable decrease as the values of the other variable increase. In the bridge-length experiment, the relationship between length and breaking weight was an inverse variation.

variación inversa Una relación no lineal en la que el producto de dos variables es constante. Una variación inversa se puede representar por una ecuación de la forma $y = \frac{k}{x}$, ó $xy = k$, donde k es una constante. En una variación inversa, los valores de una variable disminuyen a medida que los valores de la otra variable aumentan. En el experimento de la longitud de los puentes, la relación entre la longitud y el peso de colapso era una variación inversa.

L

linear relationship A relationship in which there is a constant rate of change between two variables. A linear relationship can be represented by a straight-line graph and by an equation of the form $y = mx + b$. In the equation, m is the slope of the line, and b is the y-intercept.

relación líneal Una relación en la que hay una tasa de cambio constante entre dos variables. Una relación lineal se puede representar por una gráfica de línea recta y por una ecuación de la forma $y = mx + b$. En la ecuación, m es la pendiente de la recta y b es el intercepto y.

Notes _____

_____

_____

_____

mathematical model An equation or a graph that describes, at least approximately, the relationship between two variables. In this unit, mathematical models are made by acquiring data, plotting the data points, and, when the points showed a pattern, finding an equation or curve that fits the trend in the data. A mathematical model allows you to make reasonable guesses for values between and sometimes beyond the data points.

modelo matemático Una ecuación o una gráfica que describe, al menos aproximadamente, la relación entre dos variables. En esta unidad, los modelos matemáticos se hacen obteniendo datos, trazando los puntos de los datos y, cuando los puntos muestran un patrón, hallando la ecuación o curva que muestra la tendencia de los datos. Un modelo matemático permite hacer estimaciones razonables para los valores entre y, a veces, fuera de los puntos de los datos.

multiplicative inverses Two numbers, a and b, that satisfy the equation $ab = 1$. For example, 3 and $\frac{1}{3}$ are multiplicative inverses, and $-\frac{1}{2}$ and -2 are multiplicative inverses.

inversos multiplicativos Dos números, a y b, que cumplen con la ecuación $ab = 1$. Por ejemplo, 3 y $\frac{1}{3}$ son inversos multiplicativos, y $-\frac{1}{2}$ y -2 son inversos multiplicativos.

Notes

Academic Vocabulary

Academic vocabulary words are words that you see in textbooks and on tests. These are not math vocabulary terms, but knowing them will help you succeed in mathematics.

Las palabras de vocabulario académico son palabras que ves en los libros de texto y en las pruebas. Éstos no son términos de vocabulario de matemáticas, pero conocerlos te ayudará a tener éxito en matemáticas.

D

describe To explain or tell in detail. A written description can contain facts and other information needed to communicate your answer. A diagram or a graph may also be included.
related terms: express, explain, illustrate

Sample: Describe the relationship between hours worked and pay.

Hours Worked	1	2	3
Total Pay	$5.50	$11.00	$16.50

The relationship is linear. Total pay varies directly with the number of hours worked. That is, as the number of hours worked increases by one, the pay increases by $5.50. This means that the employee earns $5.50 for each hour worked. I can also draw a graph that shows this relationship.

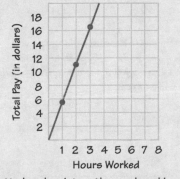

I plotted each point on the graph and I drew one line through all of the points. I can also write an equation, $P = 5.5t$, where P is the amount of money earned and t is the number of hours worked to represent this relationship.

describir Explicar o decir con detalle. Una descripción escrita puede contener hechos y otra información necesaria para comunicar tu respuesta. También se puede incluir un diagrama o una gráfica.
términos relacionados: expresar, explicar, ilustrar

Ejemplo: Describe la relación entre las horas trabajadas y el pago.

Horas trabajadas	1	2	3
Pago total	$5.50	$11.00	$16.50

La relación es lineal. El pago total varía directamente con el número de horas trabajadas. Es decir, a medida que el número de horas trabajadas aumenta en uno, el pago aumenta en $5.50 dólares. Esto significa que el empleado gana $5.50 por cada hora trabajada. También puedo dibujar una gráfica que muestre esta relación.

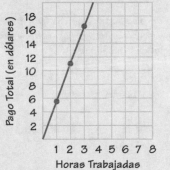

Marqué cada punto en la gráfica y tracé una línea a través de todos los puntos. Para representar esta relación, también puedo escribir una ecuación, $P = 5.5t$, donde P es la cantidad de dinero ganado y t es el número de horas trabajadas.

Notes _____

_____

_____

_____

Ⓔ

explain To give facts and details that make an idea easier to understand. Explaining can involve a written summary supported by a diagram, chart, table, or a combination of these.

related terms: analyze, clarify, describe, justify, tell

Sample: The equation $c = 75d + 15$ gives the charge c in dollars for renting a car for d days. Explain what the numbers and variables in the equation represent.

> The variable c represents the total amount the customer is charged. The variable d is the number of days the car is rented. 75 is the cost per day of renting the car. 15 is an additional one-time fee for the customer.

explicar Dar hechos y detalles que hacen que una idea sea más fácil de comprender. Explicar puede implicar un resumen escrito apoyado por un diagrama, una gráfica, una tabla o una combinación de éstos.

términos relacionados: analizar, aclarar, describir, justificar, decir

Ejemplo: La ecuación $c = 75d + 15$ da el cargo c en dólares por rentar un auto por d días. Explica qué representan los números y las variables en la ecuación.

> La variable c representa la cantidad total que se le cobra al cliente. La variable d es el número de días que se rentó el automóvil. 75 es el costo por día de rentar el auto. 15 es una cuota adicional única para el cliente.

Ⓢ

solve To determine the value or values that makes a given statement true. Several methods and strategies can be used to solve a problem including estimating, isolating the variable, drawing a graph, or using a table of values.

related terms: calculate, find

Sample: Solve the equation $8x - 16 = 12$ for x.

> I can solve the equation by isolating x on the left side of the equation.
> $8x - 16 = 12$
> $8x = 28$
> $x = \frac{28}{8} = \frac{7}{2} = 3.5$
>
> I also can also sketch a graph of $y = 8x - 16$. When $y = 12$, x is between 3 and 4, so I know my solution is reasonable.

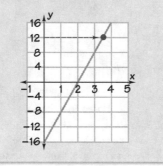

resolver Determinar el valor o valores que hacen cierto un enunciado dado. Pueden usarse varios métodos y estrategias para resolver un problema incluyendo estimar, despejar la variable, dibujar una gráfica o usar una tabla de valores.

términos relacionados: calcular, hallar

Ejemplo: Resuelve la ecuación $8x - 16 = 12$ para hallar el valor de x.

> Puedo resolver la ecuación despejando x en el lado izquierdo de la ecuación.
> $8x - 16 = 12$
> $8x = 28$
> $x = \frac{28}{8} = \frac{7}{2} = 3.5$
>
> También puedo hacer el bosquejo de una gráfica de $y = 8x - 16$. Cuando $y = 12$, x está entre 3 y 4, así que sé que mi solución es razonable.

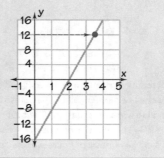

68 Thinking with Mathematical Models

Notes _____

_____

_____

_____

Index

STUDENT PAGE

Notes _____

_____

_____

_____

Acknowledgments

Team Credits

The people who made up the **Connected Mathematics 2** team —representing editorial, editorial services, design services, and production services— are listed below. Bold type denotes core team members.

Leora Adler, Judith Buice, Kerry Cashman, Patrick Culleton, Sheila DeFazio, Katie Hallahan, Richard Heater, **Barbara Hollingdale, Jayne Holman,** Karen Holtzman, **Etta Jacobs,** Christine Lee, Carolyn Lock, Catherine Maglio, **Dotti Marshall,** Rich McMahon, Eve Melnechuk, Kristin Mingrone, Terri Mitchell, **Marsha Novak,** Irene Rubin, Donna Russo, Robin Samper, Siri Schwartzman, **Nancy Smith,** Emily Soltanoff, **Mark Tricca,** Paula Vergith, Roberta Warshaw, Helen Young

Additional Credits

Diana Bonfilio, Mairead Reddin, Michael Torocsik, nSight, Inc.

Technical Illustration

WestWords, Inc.

Cover Design:

tom white.images

Photos

2 t, Jay S. Simon/Getty Images, Inc.; **2 b,** Jeff Greenberg/Alamy; **3,** Photodisc/Getty Images, Inc.; **5,** Kaluzny-Thatcher/Getty Images, Inc.; **7,** Javier Larrea/AGE Fotostock; **9,** Simon DesRochers/Masterfile; **14,** Jay S. Simon/Getty Images, Inc.; **16,** Richard Haynes; **21,** Richard Haynes; **26,** Galen Rowell/Corbis; **31,** Jeff Greenberg/Alamy; **34,** Ron Kimball/Ron Kimball Stock; **37,** PictureQuest; **41,** Richard Haynes; **42,** SuperStock, Inc./SuperStock; **45,** Bob Daemmrich/PhotoEdit; **50,** Yellow Dog Productions/Getty Images, Inc.; **51,** Macduff Everton/Corbis; **54,** AP Photo/Keystone/Steffen Schmidt; **55,** Richard Haynes; **57,** Richard Haynes; **59,** Dennis MacDonald/PhotoEdit; **63,** Photodisc/Getty Images, Inc.

Data Sources

The information on the average weights for chihuahuas on page 34 is from The Complete Chihuahua Encyclopedia by Hilary Harmar. Published by Arco Reprints, 1973.
The information on the average growth of pigs on page 62 is from "Your 4H Hog Market Project," Iowa State University, University Extension, January, 1922.

Note: Every effort has been made to locate the copyright owner of the material reprinted in this book. Omissions brought to our attention will be corrected in subsequent editions.

Notes _____

_____

_____

_____

Centimeter Grid Paper

Inch Grid Paper

....

Name _____ Date _____ Class _____

Labsheet 2ACE Exercise 3

Thinking With Mathematical Models

Try to draw a line that fits each set of data as closely as possible.
Describe the strategies you used.

Graph A   **Graph B**   **Graph C**

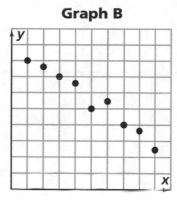

Now try these.

Graph D   **Graph E**   **Graph F**

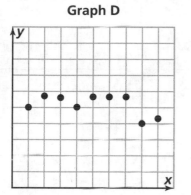
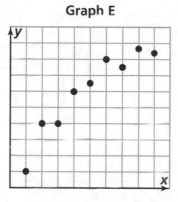

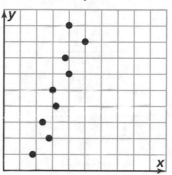

Graph G   **Graph H**   **Graph I**

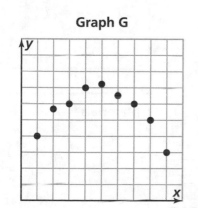
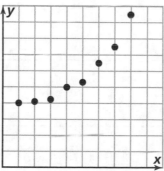
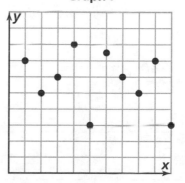

© Pearson Education, Inc., publishing as Pearson Prentice Hall. All rights reserved.

85

PACING: _____

Mathematical Goals

_____

_____

_____

_____

Launch

_____

_____

_____

_____

_____

_____

Materials

Explore

_____

_____

_____

_____

_____

_____

Materials

Summarize

_____

_____

_____

_____

_____

Materials

Glossary

Glossary

A

additive inverses Two numbers, a and b, that satisfy the equation $a + b = 0$. For example, 3 and -3 are additive inverses, and $\frac{1}{2}$ and $-\frac{1}{2}$ are additive inverses.

I

inequality A statement that two quantities are not equal. The symbols $>$, $<$, $\geq$, and $\leq$ are used to express inequalities. For example, if a and b are two quantities, then "a is greater than b" is written as $a > b$, and "a is less than b" is written as $a < b$. The statement $a \geq b$ means "a is greater than or equal to b." The statement $a \leq b$ means that "a is less than or equal to b."

inverse variation A nonlinear relationship in which the product of two variables is constant. An inverse variation can be represented by an equation of the form $y = \frac{k}{x}$, or $xy = k$, where k is a constant.

In an inverse variation, the values of one variable decrease as the values of the other variable increase. In the bridge-length experiment, the relationship between length and breaking weight was an inverse variation.

L

linear relationship A relationship in which there is a constant rate of change between two variables. A linear relationship can be represented by a straight-line graph and by an equation of the form $y = mx + b$. In the equation, m is the slope of the line, and b is the y-intercept.

M

mathematical model An equation or a graph that describes, at least approximately, the relationship between two variables. In this unit, mathematical models are made by acquiring data, plotting the data points, and, when the points showed a pattern, finding an equation or curve that fits the trend in the data. A mathematical model allows you to make reasonable guesses for values between and sometimes beyond the data points.

multiplicative inverses Two numbers, a and b, that satisfy the equation $ab = 1$. For example, 3 and $\frac{1}{3}$ are multiplicative inverses, and $-\frac{1}{2}$ and -2 are multiplicative inverses.

Index

Acknowledgments

Team Credits

The people who made up the **Connected Mathematics 2** team—representing editorial, editorial services, design services, and production services—are listed below. Bold type denotes core team members.

Leora Adler, Judith Buice, Kerry Cashman, Patrick Culleton, Sheila DeFazio, Richard Heater, **Barbara Hollingdale, Jayne Holman,** Karen Holtzman, **Etta Jacobs,** Christine Lee, Carolyn Lock, Catherine Maglio, **Dotti Marshall,** Rich McMahon, Eve Melnechuk, Kristin Mingrone, Terri Mitchell, **Marsha Novak,** Irene Rubin, Donna Russo, Robin Samper, Siri Schwartzman, **Nancy Smith,** Emily Soltanoff, **Mark Tricca,** Paula Vergith, Roberta Warshaw, Helen Young

Additional Credits

Diana Bonfilio, Mairead Reddin, Michael Torocsik, nSight, Inc.

Technical Illustration

Schawk, Inc.

Cover Design

tom white.images

DATE DUE